Are You Serious?

Are You Serious?

An Illustrated Collection of Things That Suck.

Sean Stadler

Library of Congress Cataloging-in-Publication Data

Stadler, Sean
Are You Serious? An Illustrated Collection of Things That
Suck/
Sean Stadler.
p. cm.
ISBN: 978-0-615-39023-9

1. American wit and humor. I. Title.

This book is a list of things that piss me off. One day, I complained so much that some guy said, "Hey asshole, why don't you go write a book about it?" So I did. This book has no categories or rankings and is not meant to be read in sequence. Eventually someone looking for attention will probably come along and ask why I didn't write a book about positive, realistic solutions for society's problems instead of just mindlessly complaining about them. I can only imagine how fucking boring that would be. Cheers.

Chapter 1

I hate it how a group of people will hear slightly different weather forecasts and become attached to those predictions as if they'd researched everything themselves. Then when a conversation starts, they all get defensive about the predictions they heard.

Fred: "So, we're supposed to get ten to sixteen inches of snow, and it's going to start around four."

Linda: "No, it will be eight to twelve inches, and it's going to hit around seven."

Barney: "I always know snow's coming when my face starts to twitch and my balls go numb. Actually, the same thing happens after drinking moonshine. Come to think of it, I don't believe that has much to do with snow at all."

Who's in charge of packaging these days? Anything I buy now is in a clear plastic container that's been welded shut. Any of you assholes think about how I'm supposed to get this thing open? People should go to jail for this. Then we can observe how well they can weld their cheeks shut in the shower.

Have you ever been on an airplane when the wheels touch down and suddenly everyone bursts into applause? Who claps when a plane lands? That's the guy's job! Did you think the odds were against a safe landing? Same goes for people who clap in a theatre when the movie ends. Who are you clapping for? The kid in the projection booth? He's probably so high he doesn't know where he is to start with. I bet you applaud the paint on your house when it dries.

Home shopping networks claim it's a convenience to shop at home. Memo to asshole: You'd save even more money if you only bought things you needed before some jerk-off on TV said you did.

Infomercials for abdominal machines. One or two designs are ok, but not all of them can walk on water. So shut your mouths, put on some shirts, and get some real jobs.

When you're at a bowling alley and some eight-year-old winds up and launches a ball in a six-foot arc that crashes down on the lane like a wrecking ball.

When you go to a movie and so many advertisements and previews play before the show that you forget what movie you went to go see.

Animal lovers who say that sense of smell makes animals superior to humans. I watch a documentary on TV, or listen to some expert about how humans have neglected their sense of smell over the eons and have relied too heavily on sight, whereas animals can smell a human being seven miles away, or under water, blah, blah, blah . . . You know what? Why don't you take a walk down to the zoo, look in a cage, and see who's standing on which side of the bars. I'd say we're doing pretty well for ourselves.

At the end of a movie when they launch into some sequence of explanations for what happened to all the characters instead of just ending the stupid movie that wasn't worth watching in the first place.

Public bathrooms that have automatic toilet flushers, automatic sink sensors, automatic paper towel dispensers, and a door handle that looks like something Oscar the Grouch never wiped from his ass.

Why does Detroit still get a nationally televised football game every Thanksgiving? It would be more amusing to watch a dog bark at leaves blowing in the wind for three hours than sit through an entire Lions game. I know they were one of the first teams to play on Thanksgiving, but firsts don't necessarily mean something should be repeated. Try sitting through more than ten minutes of a *Major League* sequel.

Rollerbladers who take themselves seriously enough to consider wind shear while dressing.

Anyone who refers to the Dave Matthews Band as "Dave" and honestly expects me to know who they're talking about without further explanation.
    "Oh my Gawwwd, Dave is playing in the park next week!"
    "Dave? I thought he had to stay a thousand feet away from playgrounds."
    "Not that Dave."

When someone is telling a funny story and he gets to the end and starts laughing so hard that he can't say the punch line, and everyone else just stands around looking at each other.

When you're driving slowly in an SUV, so you don't roll over on a winding road, and some guy in a sedan is up your ass the whole time as if you're going slow because you want to.

When you go to a bathroom at a sporting event and there are guys standing at the urinals for three and four minutes each. Obviously, they're not pissing, because even after six beers no one's going to go longer than a minute and a half. So what are they doing? Did they fall asleep? Honestly, it's one of the few problems that can't be solved with more beer.

Fast food burgers and sandwiches that are too tall to fit in my mouth.

Full-service gas pumps are a waste of space. Can you believe there are full-grown adults in this country who don't know how to pump their own gas because of this? I think that one alone cancels out Springsteen, Jersey.

When you spit out toothpaste and it hits the faucet head.

People who feel sorry for boxers with brain injuries who can't think straight after they retire. What did you expect?

Those stupid xenon headlights on cars. Whenever an Audi or a BMW is driving behind me now, it looks like the guy's flashing his brights whenever he hits a bump in the road. Naturally, I look back to see if a door's open, or if I left my coffee on the roof. Then I realize the prick probably doesn't even have a clue since he's already occupied by his state-of-the-art GPS tracker, hands-free voice-activated phone, satellite high-definition radio, and no-touch road-head mannequin.

When a professional sports team from North America plays teams only from the United States and Canada, wins a championship, and declares itself "World Champion."

What is the "Ins" key on computers that's always being hit? The letters "OVR" light up at the bottom of the screen, and you keep on typing, not aware that the whole time you're actually overwriting entire finished sentences. How did this fantastic idea ever leave the drawing board in the first place?

Stop-sign graffiti. You know those clever people who spray-paint words underneath "stop" so it reads "Stop war," or "Stop unions," or "Stop capitalism." I mean, it's an idea with potential, but so far no one's really hit the nail on the head. How about "Stop cheapskates," or "Stop mooches," or "Stop looking like you deserve a tip, all you did was hand me a paper towel"?

Why are there never fewer than three remote controls for any TV anymore? I go to someone's house, and he says, "Make yourself at home." OK, but I have no clue how to turn on the TV. Even if I do get it on, I can't for the life of me figure out how to change the channel, fix the volume, or order dirty movies under your name. Most of the time, I just end up watching QVC for six or seven minutes before getting up to find your booze.

Joggers who wear spandex suits. Look, if I wanted to throw up while driving, I could just plug my exhaust pipe. At least the fumes would let me hallucinate about something more pleasant-looking than the contour of your ass crack.

The concept of a man getting hit in the crotch has long lost its comic appeal. Everywhere you look now on TV, when the writers run into a dead-end they turn to a crotch-shot rather than simply giving up.

When a kid hits a baseball at some guy, why not have it crack a kneecap, or puncture his ribcage, or shatter an eye socket? I'd even settle for a nice shot to the throat so his windpipe seals shut, and he writhes and gags for a few minutes. Anything but the cheap predictability of a smacked scrotum.

Why do birds fly south in the winter and north in the summer? Why don't the stupid things just stay in the middle and cut out all the flying?

Why do I always hear crap about putting the toilet seat down? When I use the restroom for a quick visit, it's easier if the seat is up. If you'd like it down, feel free to put it down whenever you need to go. I hear all the time about how women want equal access to all the same jobs as men, and believe me, I couldn't agree more.

Stores that put up their Christmas merchandise the day after Halloween and Valentine's Day decorations on New Year's Eve. As if people weren't depressed enough already, you overly excited marketing scum.

Cigarette companies have made some touching TV advertisements that appear to discourage children from smoking. The ads are almost heartwarming until you realize that the companies would never have produced these commercials if they weren't fully aware kids are going to smoke anyway.

When a new bag of chips is less than half full.

I guess the jerk-offs who buy hundreds of bottles of water a month wouldn't see anything wrong with this. Do I have to pay to give you the finger too?

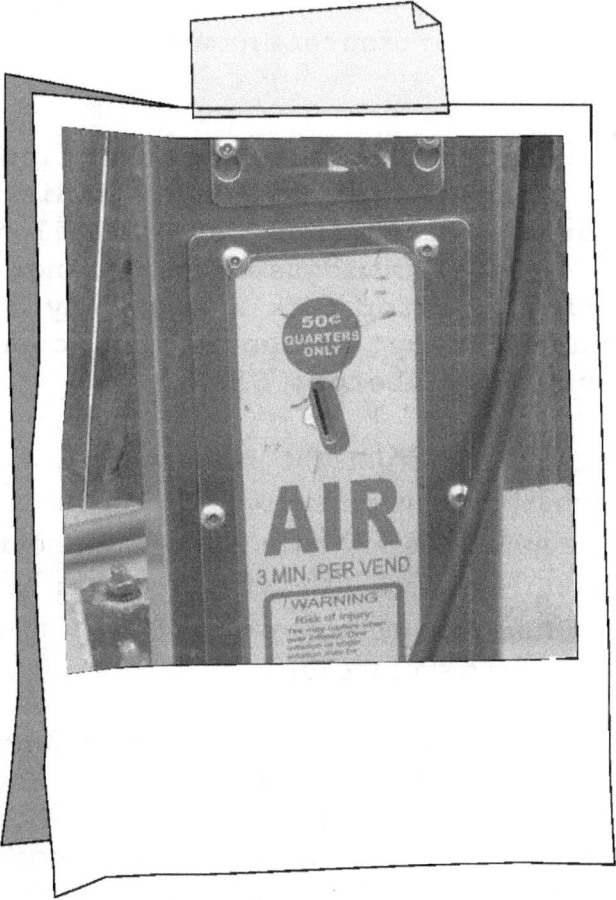

When you're staying in a hotel, and you wake up in your bed at eight-thirty in the morning. Not because of the sunshine, or a hotel wake-up call, but because the whining, screaming kids are sprinting up and down the hallway and making airplane noises, AGAIN. At this point, I'd gladly pay extra for a room door that opened outward.

Who's responsible for the size of movie drinks? I couldn't finish a "children's size" in a day, let alone a "jumbo" one. I could use those things for recycling bins for fuck's sake. Why don't you just put up a sign at the counter that says, "Diabetes: $10"?

When all six of the radio stations I have programmed into my car stereo go to commercials at the same time. It usually starts during rush hour and ends when I get home. My wrist is so tired halfway through from pressing buttons I can't even flick off anyone for the rest of the drive.

Why is it such a big event when a couple of pandas arrive at a zoo? What's so special about pandas? They're endangered? So is professional soccer, but that's not helping them much. If you're covering it because they're cute, that's not really news, and if you want to cover mating, you're about two playmates short of any television viewer's attention.

Remote controls that have been used so much that you can't read the numbers on the buttons anymore.

Political campaign advertisements on TV. They're great entertainment. Then again, it would be more realistic to just stand at a playground and watch two kids shout names, fling mud at each other's faces, and throw temper tantrums until someone did something to shut them up. In the children's case, it would be giving them candy. In the politicians' case, it would be giving them votes. You start to see a lot of consistencies if you stare at things long enough.

Why do airlines feel that the only way to handle a delay is to continually lie to their customers? Can't the airlines just tell us the pilots were caught up in a contest of tequila shots after lunch and are passed out on the men's room floor, rather than simply repeating, "We're cleaning the aircraft, and shall begin pre-boarding momentarily"?

The pretzels they sell at ballparks that are completely choked in salt, and I have to scrape it all off. Do you think I'm buying it for my damn horse?

The insecure, self-righteous people who regularly point out that "an," not "a," should be used before certain words starting with the letter "h." These are the same swine who proudly sort their recycling into seven categories, attend lectures on modern shifts in European meta-socialite behavior, and force their toddlers to read *National Geographic* before they can learn not to shit themselves. There's a reason no one talks to you.

Can we put to rest this dollar-coin bullshit? I put up with that in Europe, and my pockets weighed about four pounds each and sounded like Santa's sleigh. If I can't put it in my wallet, I don't want it. And there's no way I'm carrying around a coin purse. If you haven't noticed, I'm not an eighty-five-year-old woman.

THIS IS RIDICULOUS, WHO DESIGNS PLANE—WILL NOT PURCHASE A SECOND SEAT BEC—DESERVE TO BE ACCO—

During basketball games when a player shoots a three-pointer, and every member of the shooter's team and a dozen fools in the crowd leap to their feet and throw their arms in the air to celebrate. They're hoping the ball will go in so they can act like they called it from the start. It's great when the shot is a brick, and all the boozed-up pricks standing up have to tuck their tails between their legs, take a seat, and resume being the underwhelming people they were to begin with.

When people say something to you, but they mumble it so you ask them to repeat it, but they say the same garbled sentence as the first time. So you feel like an idiot but you bluntly ask them to tell you again, and they slow down some, but won't speak any louder. How hard is it to speak clearly? Dealing with these people is like telling an Irishman Happy Hour is over. Some things just don't register.

When a lifeguard at a water park says you can't go down any slides head-first.

I hate stall doors in public restrooms that open into the stall. This greatly increases my odds of brushing against the scum bucket as I try to squeeze out like a ferret.

When I exit a crowded store, start walking through the parking lot, and some guy starts tailing me in his car. He wants to follow me to my spot, hoping to take it when I leave. So I hear the guy creeping along, but I know my car is a good three or four hundred yards away. I almost want to turn around and tell him to keep going, but then again, it's more fun to just keep the poor bastard in suspense.

Parents who complain about violence in movies.

Why don't we just stay on daylight saving time all year round? As if it wasn't a big enough kick in the nuts to say, "Goodbye, shorts, hello, three feet of snow." You have to make the sun set eight hours before I go to sleep, too?

Weather experts who say that should you encounter a tornado while driving, instead of trying to outrun it, you should stop, get out of the car, and lie flat in a ditch. That's good to know, because there wasn't a clear line of action that came to mind when I heard about the situation.

Let me put it this way: if a tornado can follow me in a straight line down the interstate at 130 mph, then I hope it does and strips me of my pride. But if you expect me to sit in a ditch with a thumb up my ass while a wrath-of-God wind bag roars by and rips my arms off, then pass me a hit, pal, because I have to try the shit you're smoking.

When you're hitting golf balls at a driving range and you finally hit the cart that's driving around picking up balls. It's a great feeling because you think you just screwed up the guy's whole operation. Then you see him keep driving and realize that life goes on after the ball cart is hit.

Fat women who dress like they're attractive, and attractive women who complain that they're fat.

The Simpsons hasn't been funny in over ten years.

People this side of the Atlantic who don't wear deodorant.

Women who, when asked about men, say they find a sense of humor to be the most important characteristic. Give me a break. That's what everyone says. Ever hear a woman say she'd love to meet a man who knows his drinking limit but deliberately surpasses it every time? There's a keeper.

Movie critics in newspapers who sarcastically mock all but one movie on their lists, which they give four stars. This film commonly turns out to be some artistic foreign flick that's only playing in one theatre an hour and a half away about some perverted French guy who cheats on his wife for twenty years with a cow, writes a poem about it, and throws himself off a cliff. Well, I'd probably be looking for a cliff, too, if I had anything to do with that movie.

When are people going to come to their senses and stop defending Canadian geese? They're not endangered, they're not friendly, and are nothing more than pretentious, flying, long-necked rats.

I don't care much for experts' predictions on TV. Everyone is always giving his "expert" prediction about the top-five moneymaking films of the weekend, the top twenty picks in the NFL draft, or these weathermen and their daily "predictions." What good is any of it? If the person ends up being right, big fucking deal! If he's wrong, then it just proves he was full of shit, which everyone knew to begin with.

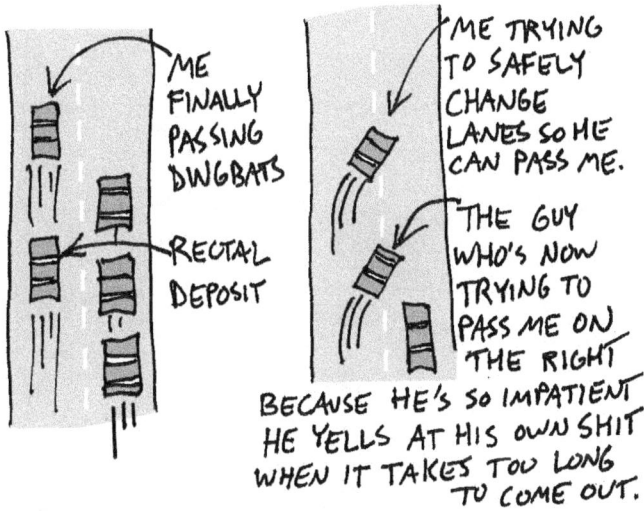

When you have only five more exits to go on the freeway and suddenly you run into a five-mile backup. After you realize there's no conceivable way to be on time where you're going, you start to think about what an impressive, mangled wreck must be causing this. Then you finally drive by the "accident," and see two cars with bent fenders and unhurt drivers smoking cigarettes. There's also a state trooper parked behind them, but he's filling out paperwork. And all of this is on the other side of the median! Then you think about how satisfied you feel: that even though it was entirely possible for all lanes of traffic to remain moving at full speed in your direction during this spectacle, the alert drivers ahead made sure you stopped to ponder the fact that you share the same evolved species as them.

People who walk their dogs without leashes. Don't think for a second I'm going to slow down for your precious, yipping sausage if it trots into the road.

Movies where you're shown the entire plot and can easily conclude the outcome after just watching the previews.

Do telemarketers just not get the picture when an entire nation hangs up on them because they called during dinner, or any time at all? Apparently not, because they keep calling, and that means someone, somewhere is buying their stuff. I've heard they prey on naïve old people. Well, why don't they stick to naïve old people and leave me the hell alone?

People who tirelessly use the word "my."

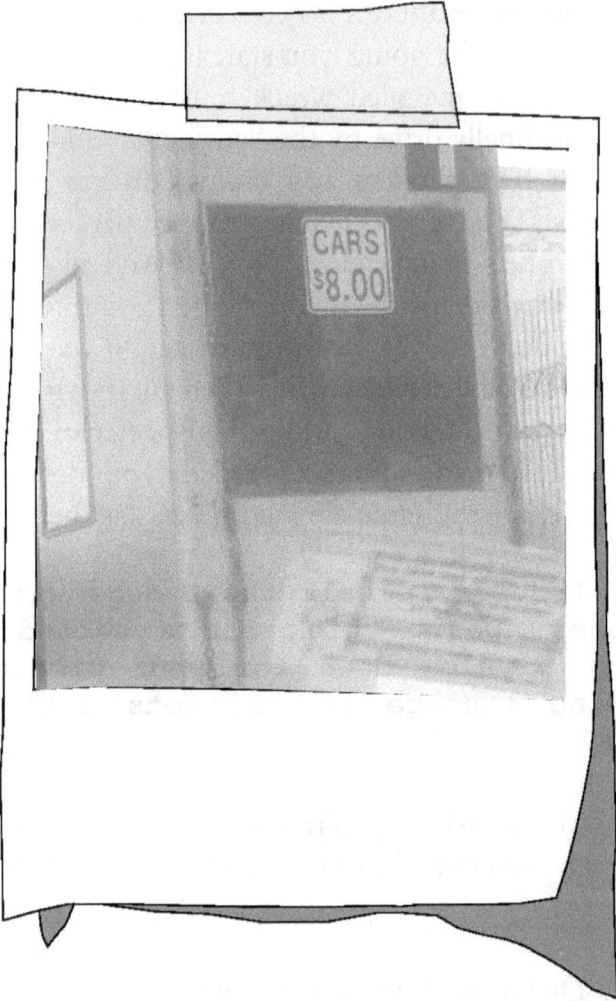

Since you're already robbing me, why not go ahead and point a gun in the window as we drive through? Scream that if I don't hand it over you'll pump a slug in my dome and feed my corpse to your rottweilers! C'mon, make it fun for the kids!

How seasons officially start before the weather changes. I'll hear some moron on the radio when there's still snow on the ground and announce that spring starts the next day. Listen, pal, spring starts when I no longer see my breath and don't have to dump coffee on my windshield just to melt the ice.

Why are sixteen year olds allowed to obtain a license to operate the statistically most deadly machine ever assembled by humankind, but they aren't allowed to watch an R-rated movie?

Pedestrians who walk into the street like they own the road and expect me to stop for them need to learn a valuable lesson: Roads were built for cars, so either wait on the curb and go buy a lottery ticket, or march right into my path, because either way you're looking at about the same odds of going home a happy camper that night.

When you cut into your steak at a restaurant and find a piece of rope in it. People don't think anything of it either, because it happens at fancy restaurants. Imagine if that shit went down at McDonald's, and someone found a piece of rope in a Big Mac. Instant lawsuit! People put up with entirely too much in the name of sophistication.

What's wrong with Velcro shoes? They worked fine when I was four. Why aren't they acceptable now?

Televised parades. It's sort of like televised fireworks, but more dignified. Why don't you just get off your ass and go to the damn parade?

When you open a magazine and half a dozen "business reply" cards fall out.

Men who let their fingernails grow to a point where you have to shine a light in their eyes and make sure somebody's still home.

When the newspaper guy delivers your paper while it's raining, but you pick it up and it's soaked despite the courteous second plastic bag.

Paper grocery bags: they're just harder to carry and more likely to break. I don't know why the suits sitting behind one-way mirrors in grocery stores haven't figured out that the only function paper bags should have is concealing booze in public.

When you get out of your car and try to close the door, but it won't shut because the seatbelt is caught in the door.

Amusement parks that get upset when you sit on the railings while waiting in line. If you're so concerned about our posture, how about some fucking benches?

When you go to a baseball game, and the person throwing out the first pitch bounces the ball ten feet in front of home plate. You're telling me that this person has known about this day for months and hasn't once practiced throwing a small object fifty-five feet on the fly, but somehow still found the time to dress like a major-league schmuck?

Guys who drink milk and just let it sit there on their moustache or beard until someone points it out.

Why do people say they've never won anything before? It happens a lot on the radio.

"You've just won one thousand dollars!"

"No waaayyaaa! I've never won annnnything beforeaaaa!"

How can you never have won anything before? Little League, checkers, thumb wrestling: you had to have won something at some point. If not, just sign up for the Special Olympics and tell them you need to get one under your belt.

When there's a show on TV like *60 Minutes*, and they're interviewing some guy who speaks English so poorly you can't understand a damn word he's saying, but the producers don't use subtitles.

At baseball games when a fair ball is hit down the line and some guy who can obviously see it's in play reaches out of the stands for it anyway.

People who aren't capable of whispering. You'll be somewhere where everyone should shut up, like a speech or a movie, and some royal douche will lean over and start talking to you in a normal indoor voice about how he found gas for cheaper this week when just last week he had to pay six cents more because he didn't have his frequent gassers card, and he bought his car with the gas mileage in mind, and he doesn't want to have to drive to another gas station to get his money's worth, and…is it *really* that hard to notice that everyone in the room can hear what you're fucking saying?

Guys who wear sandals with black socks.

When you use the only dime in your pocket to make a photocopy from a book or newspaper at the library, and you find out after the copy is made that you placed the original in the wrong direction.

When a TV commercial plays for two seconds, and then gets overrun by a different commercial.

People who always have exact change.

People who blow their noses with a napkin at a restaurant and then put the napkin right there next to their plates for everyone to enjoy.

When you've been driving for a while and you keep flipping through the radio stations because nothing good is on, and when you're stopped at a traffic light you finally find a good song. Then you're so happy you've found this song that you roll down the windows and turn up the volume so everyone around you can hear how great the song is. Then about thirty seconds later, you realize it's a commercial for hot dogs, and you sink down in your seat like the jackass you are.

Does anyone else get ticked off when they interrupt a TV show you're watching for a special report and nothing happens? They zoom to a "live" press conference that hasn't even started yet, and a bunch of people are standing around an empty podium. It takes ten minutes for someone to even come out and announce the news, and you find out it's something you don't give a shit about, like they caught a transsexual rapist who was attacking house pets in some city forty-five minutes away. Then when they finally cut back to the show you were watching, they don't even start from where it left off! So you change the channel in frustration just to flip through fifteen consecutive channels and see the same picture on all of them of the transsexual cat-rapist.

When did it become acceptable for people to announce they "have to go pee?" Why can't you just say you're "going to the bathroom"? Leave something to the imagination.

When you work on someone else's computer and the mouse is set to a really slow speed, so in order to move the cursor from one end of the screen to the other you have to physically pick up the mouse and move it across the desk two or three times. The sensitivity of every mouse should be set so the cursor moves from one end of the screen to the other based on how far a wrist can swivel in a single motion; it's the same principle on which male body parts were designed, and that's worked out pretty well so far.

When you're in a hurry to get somewhere but happen to notice there's a new voicemail on your cell phone, so you try to listen to it quickly and hear, "You have two saved voice messages. You have one new voice message. You have six messages marked for deletion. First message marked for deletion, received last April at eight twenty-two p.m. . . ."

People who leave campaign bumper stickers on their cars after an election just to broadcast the fact that they voted for the other person, and personally can't be held responsible for any current problems.

Unnecessary vowels in words like "Towne House," "Malte Shoppe," or "pretentious scum bague."

People who wear sunglasses indoors.

You know, even when
the day comes when I
can afford to give a car
as a Christmas present, I
won't give your brand.
That's because when I'm
forced to sit through the
exact same TV commercial
six times an hour during
a three-hour football game,
I'd rather be dragged
by one leg from the back
of a bus as my primary
form of transportation
than give you my business,
you elitist, sadistic,
shit-peddling grinch.

When a bunch of people are waiting for an elevator, and the button has already been pressed, but every special camper who joins the group has to push it again for himself.

When you put a perfectly good coin into a vending machine, and it falls right through to the change slot.

Vegetarians who claim that "meat is murder." Why do you make such a big deal about animals being killed and not the hundreds of members of your own species being murdered every day? And what have animals ever done for you? I understand if you love your dog, but who gives a fuck about a bunch of cows you've never even met? Your priorities are more diluted than an open Coors Light at the bottom of a swimming pool.

How soda companies relentlessly bombard me with flashy new advertisements year in and year out. Look, I'm not going to drink your product because a celebrity tells me to. I drink your competitor's product because it tastes better.

People who blow their noses, then look into the Kleenex to see what came out.

When you're driving your car and a passenger helps himself to your volume knob. I'll put up with trash on the floor, or feet out the window, but don't you going playing with fire.

How about these cars with turn signals built into the rearview mirrors? It's harder to see a signal there than it is by the taillights, so what's the point? If any of the pricks who bought these cars actually used turn signals in the first place, other than to show off the new blinkers, then we could all save a lot of time and effort wasted by giving them the finger.

When you get up for a snack and grab a box of donut holes or Oreos, but you want to be health-conscious so you read the nutrition information first. You note that it's only 120 calories and decide that's a satisfactory amount. So you start popping the suckers into your mouth, and around eighteen or twenty, you glance at the side of the box and realize the serving size is two, and that you just consumed two thousand calories in the last eight minutes.

When you watch a fat guy squeeze a bottle of ketchup on his food and it makes a sound resembling the bowel movement he probably had earlier that day, and you can't help but visualize the connection.

There are too many shows about tough-beat cops who sweat it out on the streets to fight crime and depress viewers by focusing solely on human scum and tough-guy police banter for an hour. Why not give them a partner on Prozac who draws smiley faces on chalk-body outlines once in a while?

Backseat drivers with the patience of a four year old and the driving sense of the shit stain in its pants.

Does anyone know the name of any stadium anymore? Joe Robbie Stadium became Pro Player Park became Dolphinsafetuna.com Athletic Complex. You do realize that fans aren't going to say "Fed-Ex Orange Bowl" or "TD Banknorth Garden" just because you think they should. They'll say "The Orange Bowl", "The Garden", or just plain "meet me at the game." In other words, even if your corporate name is seen by a lot of people, that doesn't mean anyone gives a shit. It is nothing more than another inconvenient advertisement, and it will be treated like one, too.

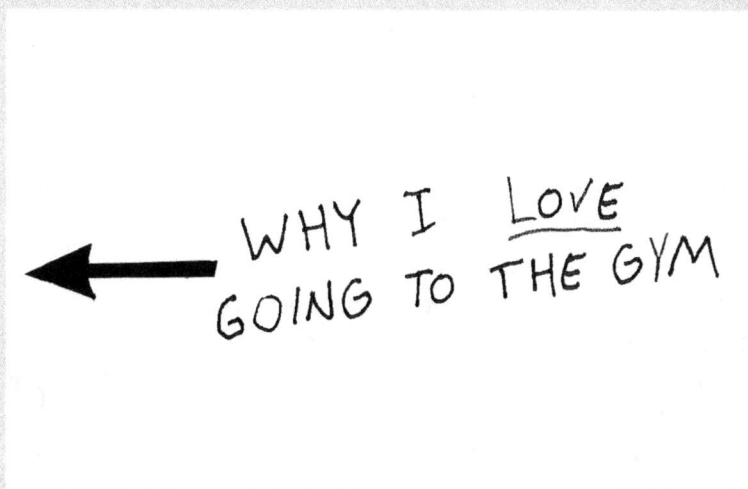

←— WHY I LOVE GOING TO THE GYM

When you spend all the energy you have left to get up from the couch to find something to eat, and all that's left in the refrigerator is old Chinese food, half a bottle of mayo, an empty jar of pickles, and you actually stand there contemplating what to eat.

Why is spaghetti so popular? It's so long you have to spend two or three minutes cutting it into manageable pieces that aren't even manageable. Then if you're finally able to slurp it into your mouth, the sauce squirts everywhere. The whole thing is about as practical as an intervention on St. Patrick's Day.

Before every Olympics, why do the media hype up all the new events, then never cover a single one? Why do they think I only care about track and field and basketball? I want to see four-foot-tall teenagers in trampoline jumping. I want to see two Asian guys playing Ping-Pong thirty feet back from the table. I want to see some jacked-up mutant from Scandinavia try to lift 10,000 pounds with his crotch. Let me tell you why I don't watch the Olympics: because I want to watch what I find entertaining, not what Nike tells me is.

When you've been holding a newspaper and don't realize your hands are covered in ink until you've finger-painted a half dozen walls around the house.

When a doctor says something will feel "a little uncomfortable." That's because according to doctors' relative sense of pain, they're likely to say something "won't hurt at all" whether they're testing your reflexes or feeding your leg into a snow blower.

When an event takes place like a submarine collides with a giant squid or some politician texts pictures of his genitals to a staff member, and every news station covers it nonstop for at least a week. None of them seem to anticipate that viewers will become violently sick of this story after ten minutes, and no one wants to hear about it. There should be one news station devoted to covering absolutely everything except the "big" story that's plaguing the other networks like a bad case of Tijuana tap water.

People with coffee breath who don't realize it, don't give a damn, or probably just smell bad to begin with.

Who picks what fashions are "hot" or "in" for any given season? They actually have a special report on the news telling me what I'm supposed to wear for the next three months. They also bring on a "fashion expert" to discuss the matter, and allow this person to talk unimpeded on camera upwards of a minute without anyone bludgeoning their head with a blunt object.

When you buy a tray full of nachos at a game and the cheese runs out after only half the chips are gone.

When you're buying something at a cash register and the cashier gives you bills on the bottom, receipt in the middle, and coins on top. Isn't it pretty? Maybe, but it's a pain in the ass. That's because I have to put down the bag I've just been handed, put the bills into that hand, and pour the coins in my pocket. Then I need to crumple the receipt and throw it away, followed by stuffing the bills into my wallet. Finally, I can pick up my bag again, and be on my way.

Listen, coins on bottom, bills on top, and put the receipt on rye with cheese and have it for lunch for all I care. If something was worth enough for me to give a damn, I wouldn't have paid in cash.

Airline headsets when the audio comes and goes in one side of the headset the entire movie.

TV shows like *World's Most Amazing Police Chases* where they show every clip during the introduction so there's nothing new left to watch during the show itself.

When you're playing miniature golf and there's some family with four kids, all younger than ten years old, playing in front of you. Then every time you finish a hole, you have to sit on a bench for fifteen minutes until the youngest kid who's shorter than his own putter taps the ball in for a twenty-nine.

I can't stand it when a car company says its car was rated the best in its class. It doesn't say much when, later, the commercial says the car is in a class by itself.

Major League pitchers who can't hit well. Can you give me one reason why they can't be good at hitting? They work only once every five days, so why can't they get in the cage and hit a few balls the rest of the time? With all that time to improve, you'd think they'd be the best hitters out there! Instead, they're content shuffling out to the bullpen, sticking a finger in their ears, and counting the zeros in their paychecks every half inning.

How car models come out nine months before the year they're named for: the 2012 Toyota Accelerator will come out in March of 2011, and it will have already won awards by that April!

When you get a soda can at a vending machine, and there's dirt on the rim where your mouth's supposed to go. Are you growing the fucking things in your backyard? For one dollar, you'd think I could get a minimal effort at sanitation.

Signs on the road that say "Speed checked by radar." Well, no shit, how else would they do it?

When you're descending over neighborhoods in an airplane, and look out the window to realize that everyone else has a swimming pool but you.

People who always smile for photographs. How boring is that? You should have to show the face of however you're feeling at the moment the picture is taken. That would be much more interesting, especially if two people just had a fight. They should have to put their hands around each other's throats, too.

People who ask to see photos of another person's baby. Whenever a couple has a kid, the parents start winging pictures around like Frisbees on 4/20. If you're like me and think all babies look pretty much the same, one way to ease the pain is to look for distinguishing features that will likely be the punch line of grade school humor for years to come. Then smile and tell the parents what a winner they have, all the while picturing a fat kid taking the brunt of a future dodge ball massacre.

How any golf tournament, even in its first year, can be called a "Classic."

Men who wear giant rings. You want me to notice that thing on your finger? You were on a high school state championship football team? I'm sure you get admiration from complete strangers who defer to your superiority over them for this achievement. Hey, unless your name is Bundy and you went to Polk High, I don't want to hear about it.

Cell phones that are so small the part you're supposed to speak into is four inches away from your mouth.

When you have to slow down while driving to swerve past a jogger who's running in the road next to a perfectly usable sidewalk.

When you notice the batteries are dying on your TV remote but you're too lazy to change them, so you hope that if you just keep hitting the buttons harder it'll somehow work forever.

When two people stand side-by-side and block an escalator so you can't pass them.

Who applauds themselves? You ever hear people say, "Give yourself a hand"? Or these athletes and movie stars who win awards and then clap with everyone else when they get up on stage? To have hundreds of people applauding your mere presence and feeling the need to join in makes me wonder what kind of self-esteem crisis this douche bag must be enduring.

Jar Jar Binks.

When you start feeling hungry while driving on a highway, and you see a sign for McDonald's at exit 78. So you get off the exit and the damn place ends up being five miles and an oil change away from the interstate. It should be a law that your restaurant must be visible from the highway to be listed on a highway sign.

When you're sitting in an airport terminal waiting to get on a plane, and they announce that boarding is about to take place for people sitting in rows twenty-nine through forty-five. So at this point, all the people waiting for the plane (every single person) cram to the front of the line, and hold out their tickets like they all have a legitimate chance of boarding then.

When you're at the grocery store pushing a cart down the aisle, pretending like it's a race car, and you turn a corner, and someone's standing right there. Then you have to stop on a dime and act like you weren't pretending it was a race car.

When it comes to new ideas on television, why is the inevitable response to a successful show to drive the concept into the ground? One hit takes the lead, and the spin-offs fall in line on cue. *Law & Order*, *CSI*, and the whole make ten people live together and see what happens bit have pretty much fizzled out. Everything that could be given a makeover has been, and I'm patiently awaiting the first plug for *America's Next Top Apathetic Government Employee*. How about a show where they just pull some guy out of jail and beat the shit out of him for a half hour? Simple, satisfying, and to-the-point entertainment.

Have you ever been filling your car up with gas and looked down to see the sign that says, "Please do not top off." So you top it off just to spite the sign, and gas comes pouring down the side of your car? Then you're so bitter that the sign won that you don't even clean off the gas. You just put in the cap and drive away.

People who write "Wash me" on the backs of their own dirty cars.

FEE NOTICE,
THE OWNER OF THIS TERMINAL ADDS
TO CASH WITHDRAWALS (AND CREDIT CARD CASH
ADVANCES, IF APPLICABLE) A TERMINAL
USAGE FEE OF $3.00
THIS CHARGE IS IN ADDITION TO ANY FEE
WHICH MAY BE ASSESSED BY YOUR FINANCIAL
INSTITUTION

WOULD YOU LIKE TO CONTINUE?

PRESS IF YES ------------->

PRESS IF NO ------------->

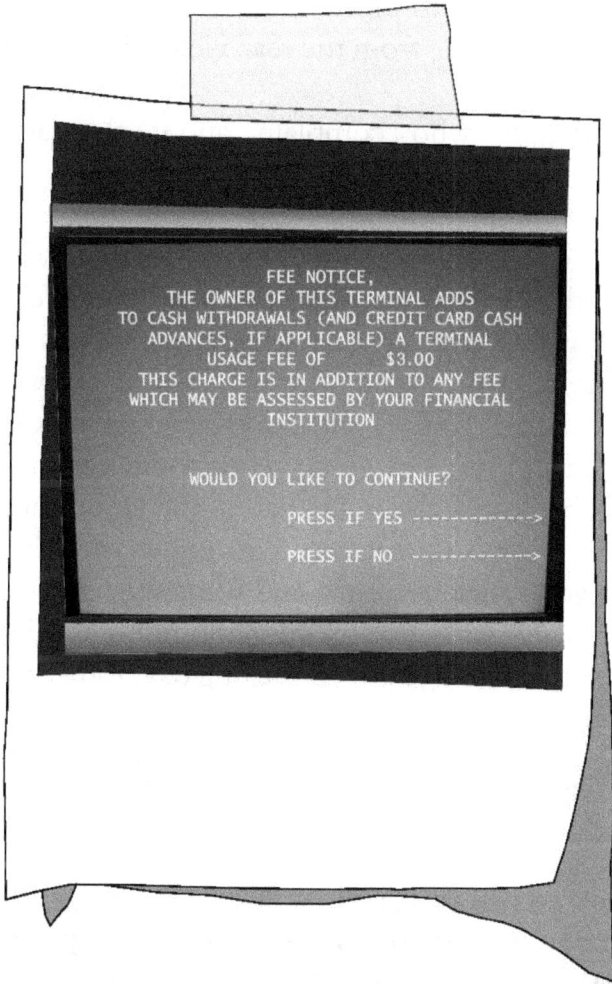

Great! Now which button removes your cock from my ass?

Anyone with more than five Christmas tree air fresheners hanging from the rear-view mirror in his car.

People who complain about the price of cigarettes.

For all of you anal-compulsive people who feel the need to travel from one event in your life to the next, bowling over anyone who might inconvenience you, the next time one of you honks at me within a quarter-second of the light changing green, here's what I'm going to do: I'm going to turn the car off, walk around back, pull down my pants, and sit on the trunk with my thumb up my ass. You know why? Because you've got a stick up yours, and someone has to let you know what your major malfunction in life is. Honk all you want, 'cause I've got all fucking day. Ride that stick good and hard: it's gonna be a while.

Why do movie theatres always make a big deal during the previews that they gave you a nice, cushioned seat and a drink holder? That's expected of movie theatres these days. For $12 a pop, a lap dance isn't out of the question, either.

When the TV's on mute and something important like the final score of "World's Strongest Man" is blocked by the word "mute" on the screen. So you race around looking for the remote to turn up the volume, but by the time you actually run to the TV itself, they've taken the score off the screen.

When a sick person coughs around you without even making an attempt to cover his or her mouth.

When you're watching the introduction to *The Simpsons*, and you start to read what Bart's writing on the blackboard, but they cut away before you finish.

When you're walking along the side of an outdoor swimming pool, and you stub your toe on an uneven crack in the cement.

Why are there so many national appreciation weeks and months? What exactly are the criteria to obtain a national appreciation week? Do you actually have to fill out a form, or do you just decide that next week is National-Beer-before-Liquor-See-Who-Gets-Fired-Quicker week?

When you go to the carwash and they finish drying your car with the rags, and when you get inside it stinks because they sprayed it with air freshener that smells like a urinal cake.

When I save something on the computer, then try to exit the program, and it asks me, "Do you want to save your changes?" Didn't I just do that? You wonder how often the thing really does what you tell it to.

I hate in movies or TV shows when they rush someone to the hospital and use a defibrillator: the one where the doctor yells, "Clear!," and then shocks the person's chest. You always know when they pull that out the guy's dead. Have you ever seen a show where it works? No, never.

When I'm trying to buy a new cell phone and the salesperson keeps pushing all these "cutting-edge" models that offer hands-free technology, Internet access, GPS locater, breathalyzer, personal lubricant, and hair restraint for throwing up in a toilet. Believe it or not, unlike some of your customers, my personal life revolves around more than a piece of plastic attached to my head. If it rings, it'll do.

Why are there preseason MVPs in sports? How can you be the most valuable player before you've done anything? This is just combining past achievement with future potential into one big circle jerk of debate that means absolutely nothing. If masturbation has lost its appeal, then find something else to do soon, because at this rate you'll be speculating on national TV about which player will be the biggest postseason disappointment in the sack.

Who decided that every radio station needs a morning show? Can't some of them just play music? I'm driving along at eight in the morning, and all I hear is laughter.

"HA HA HA, John, that prank call you made sure was funny."

"HO HO HO, you got that right, Fred. It's almost enough to make you laugh just from listening to that prank call."

The last thing I want to hear when I'm half asleep is a group of people who are too cheerful, considering the hour, not to be actively snorting cocaine. Instead of happy morning shows, why not just put a microphone on a disgruntled middle-aged guy who yells a lot and hates his breakfast, his car, his commute, and pretty much other people in general. Let's listen to him wake up and go to work, so we can all do the same with a smile.

What's all this crap on the news about former reality-show contestants and what they're doing with their lives now? Do you care if one of them appears on *Jeopardy*? Do you care if they take a vacation to Europe? What's made these people's lives so interesting since they were on TV? What made them interesting when they were on TV? Why am I still talking about these people?

It is not a newsworthy story to cover where the Christmas tree for the state capitol building was cut down.

Why does every kid have ADD these days? As soon as one of them doesn't finish a test on time, must have ADD, better drug him up. Then there's ADHD, for kids who can't finish a test but also climb around the room instead of taking it. I understand there are children with legitimate medical and psychological conditions, but did it ever occur to anyone that a lot of these kids might just be the product of a steady diet of TV and processed sugar? Or perhaps if a kid can't finish a test on time, maybe he's just not that smart?

Why bother with press conferences? They're supposed to be announcements for important events? Then why is the announcement itself given out beforehand? "The NHL has called a press conference to announce hockey has been cancelled in general." Who cares once everyone already knows?

HELLO SIR, I'D LIKE TO INTRODUCE YOU TO OUR LATEST MODEL PHONE, COMPLETE WITH HANDS-FREE CAPABILITIES, ALONG WITH A NO-YEAR WARRANTY, FIVE YEARS OF FORCED LABOR, AND IF I'M NOT BEING OBNOXIOUS ENOUGH, MAY I JUST GO AHEAD AND RUB MY BARE ASS ON YOUR FACE?

I—I'M SORRY. AT WHAT POINT DID I EVER EXPRESS INTEREST IN WHATEVER IT IS YOU'RE SELLING? I WASN'T PAYING ATTENTION BECAUSE I WAS TOO BUSY FANTASIZING ABOUT HOW A VIOLENT DEATH WOULD BE MORE PLEASANT THAN LISTENING TO YOU.

TV commercials for acne medications. In the "after" picture, you still resemble a pizza, just without pepperoni.

Have you ever stayed home from work or school when you're sick and had to watch TV all day? Ever see the talk shows on in the afternoon? Ever notice how many episodes use the theme of "makeovers" for their show? Or the ones where they send troubled teens to boot camp? Ever feel like sort of a clapping monkey when after three hours of this garbage you still want more?

I'm getting tired of professional sports leagues trying to make their athletes appear as if they're spending all their free time reading to children, planting gardens, or visiting hospitals. That's not what I see on the eleven o'clock news.

How are people still being knighted these days? Doesn't it seem a little corny at this point? Singers, actors, politicians, and what did they really accomplish to deserve this? I think to achieve knighthood one should at least have to know how to joust.

Does anyone else roll his eyes when people read written apology statements at press conferences? Like when famous people get drunk, speak their minds, and piss some people off. Then they always end up apologizing, whether it sounds like they want to or not. Eventually, they may feel bad and want to apologize, but sometimes you can tell they really don't care, and their typed apology statements sound about as convincing as the story from a naked guy on a tractor pulled over for a DUI. If someone wants to apologize, then he should, but if he doesn't want to, no one should make him feel compelled to do so.

Why do people get above-ground swimming pools? It's probably as much effort to build one of those as it is to dig a hole in the ground. I thought only people who lived next to highways had them, the same people who couldn't find a single better piece of land in this entire country than next to an interstate. Do you really want to sink to that level?

Yes. The pun was intended, you clever son of a bitch.

Highway signs that tell you when you're entering or leaving a particular watershed area. If you're going to throw away money to validate an over-inflated budget, why not just put up highway signs with jokes on them? You could have a question on one sign, and the punch line a mile down the road. Late at night, you could have electronic signs that broadcast really raunchy jokes, too, after the kids are asleep. I mean, we're paying for this stuff. Make me laugh.

People who judge how far they have left to go with parallel parking by bumping into the car behind them.

When you have to multiply twelve by seven, eight, or nine in your head, and get annoyed because you never bothered to learn all the twelve times-tables.

Protesting activists who harass consumers about buying clothing products produced in sweatshops. The activists do this because they haven't figured out an effective way to stop exploitation yet, so they pass on the burden of action and consequent blame for inaction to the consumer. I've heard rumors about sweatshops, but how do I know what's true, and to what extent? That's just for specific big-name brands, too. What about the T-shirt I buy from a street vendor in Chicago?

"Sir, was this shirt produced in a sweatshop?"

"No. Twenty dollars."

What am I supposed to say?

Fans at baseball games who yell at other fans to throw back homerun balls hit by the visiting team. The only people who have the right to yell are ones who have done so themselves. Seriously, how many times are you going to catch a ball in your life? Maybe once? I'm not about to indulge the wishes of some beer-guzzling, pot-bellied piece-of-shit just for a quick round of applause. Twenty years from now, no one will be grateful, or even remember that I threw a ball back, but I can be glad that I kept it.

When a professional golfer has a two-inch putt and he only puts one foot in the proper stance, while letting the other one casually hang off to the side. Whenever he does miss one of those shots, seeing the look on his face is like Christmas morning in July.

When you sink a put in mini-golf but forget it's the last hole, and you go to get your ball, but it just ain't there.

When a water fountain's pressure is so weak you have to kiss the crud-covered nozzle to drink any water.

When you go on the bumper car ride a carnival and there's never enough room to build up any speed. So instead of releasing frustration by smashing into someone else's car, you just become more frustrated.

That's why I always go on the bumper cars right before closing time. That little punk may be able to laugh in your face when you bounce harmlessly off his fender, but the tables turn in the parking lot when he has his running shoes, and you have your truck.

How much time do you really save using a swipe stick at a gas pump instead of a credit card? We're talking about maybe five seconds, and now whenever you need gas, you'll have to waste more time searching for that station chain than you'd ever save at the pump once you find it. Not to mention, you've also become more or less a guaranteed customer of that gas station chain for the indefinite future. So, what exactly is the part that benefits you?

Why do donut makers even consider making more than one flavor of donut hole? Everyone eats the chocolate ones and leaves the rest sitting there. Then if you see an open box sitting around you get excited just to realize there aren't any chocolate ones left. There are some powdered ones, a few chocolate crumbs, and the brown ones that taste like sand from a camel's ass.

When you're riding a roller coaster with your arms up in the air, and you speed into a tunnel, and for a split second wonder if maybe one day the engineer had a margarita or two with lunch. Them arms go down mighty quick.

When someone at a deli doesn't cut your sandwich all the way through, so it's not easy to pull apart. Then you try to finesse the two halves apart but squeeze so hard that everything squirts out.

When the person singing the national anthem at a ballgame takes an extra minute and a half to put his or her own personal twist on the "land of the free, and home of the brave" part. Save it for *American Idol.*

When you walk down the street and see a table with kids selling raffle tickets. You think about crossing the street to avoid them, but then make eye contact with a kid and feel like you can't escape. So you walk past, and they ask if you'd like to support efforts to free an elephant from captivity somewhere in Africa. Then you tell them you have to stop at the ATM, keep walking, and think you're in the clear. But an hour later, you forget about the whole thing, walk past the same table again, and have to think of another excuse like you left your wallet in the car or you hate elephants and wish people made more pianos.

Why are there road signs that say "school bus stop ahead," and why are they hanging around the same spot for twenty years? I know people have bred some goofy kids in the past, but even if a kid repeats high school seven or eight times, he shouldn't still be taking a school bus at twenty-six. If so, he should be waiting for a garbage truck instead.

When you go for a run and the knot in your shoe comes undone. So you stop running, tie it in a double knot, and it still comes undone quicker than a Hollywood wedding vow.

Athletes who wear the number "0."

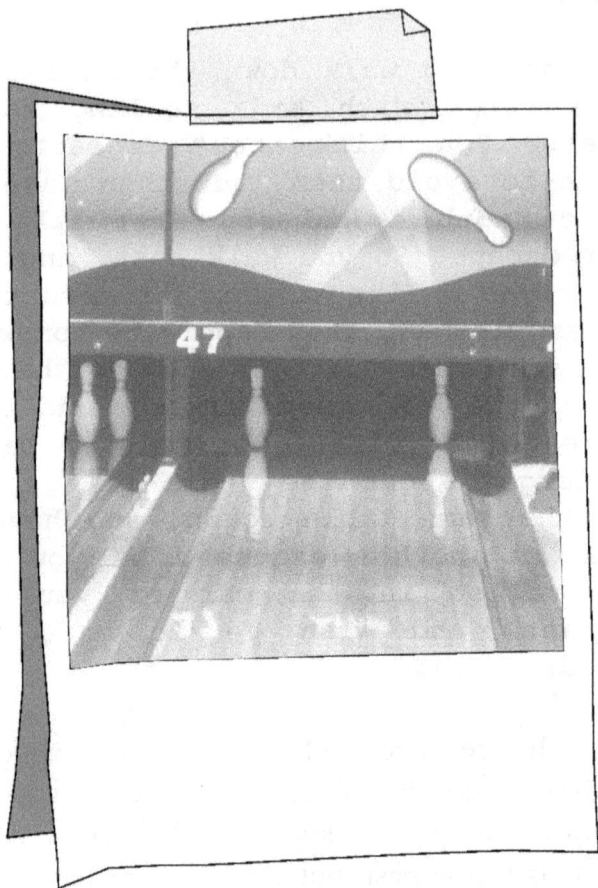

When you mark something with a bright yellow highlighter and it looks crisp and flashy, but five minutes later, it fades into an ugly orange color.

Why do computers take so long to turn on? You have to wait a good two or three minutes for the thing to wake up and scratch its nuts before it can even show you a menu. Next it'll be asking for time and a half past five o'clock.

Historical preservationists who fight to preserve buildings based on how old they are, rather than if they should ever have been built in the first place. I can understand saving Clinton's birthplace or Monica's drycleaners; it could be used for a museum someday. But if it's not going to be a museum, no one wants to buy it, and you can't see it from the road, why bother? If tomorrow I built a tool shed in the shape of a giant erect penis, and died fifty years from now, are you going to stand in front of it for the newspaper and make a serious argument to keep it? I hope so.

When you see one of those big holiday tins with three kinds of popcorn in it, and you go to eat some of the cheese or the caramel popcorn and find out the only thing left is regular popcorn.

All the people who think they've found a great ring tone for their cell phones, and who intentionally don't answer the phone whenever it rings just so you can admire their astonishing discovery.

Why do most calendars show Sunday as the first day of the week? Monday is clearly the first day of the week. They call Saturday and Sunday the weekend, not the week-partially-the-end-and-partially-the-beginning. God said it himself: he worked hard for six days and rested on the seventh. I'm not even sure how this even became an issue.

Are you like me? Do you hate it when you walk into a store at the mall and just want to look around, and three different clerks ask you in a period of three minutes whether you need help? When the third one asks, "Can I help you with anything?," I say, "Sure," and hand him my bags.

Why are there always soccer riots around the world? People are always getting crushed to death, or stadium balconies are collapsing. What makes soccer the sport for this to happen? You never hear about people getting crushed to death at a baseball or basketball game. I'm convinced it happens because everyone realizes that soccer is about as agonizing to watch as a senile old woman trying to floss the teeth of a cat that isn't there, and they all try to clear out at once. Yeah, yeah, I know it's the "beautiful" game, and it's the "world's" game, but you could say the same thing about sex. So why not just play a month-long tournament of international porn stars banging it out until there's only one left standing? Or kneeling, however things end up.

I don't care much for waiters or waitresses who try to memorize the orders at a table. It's sort of condescending in a way. We're just normal people picking ordinary meals, nothing too exotic or tough to remember. Whenever I get one of these clowns, I wait to order last and ask for something that's not on the menu, just to see how he reacts: "I'd like the roast duck and eight of your fingers in a box." Then have everyone just stare at the poor bastard.

Have you ever started watching a movie on TV late on a weeknight and you can barely stay awake about halfway through, but you want to see how it ends? So you sit there, losing interest by the minute, but can't bring yourself to turn it off after watching so much. You hope there's a scene where people start screwing in a helicopter or a guy mows down twenty people with a Gatling gun, or everyone is eaten alive, but there never is, and the movie just ends. Then you can't get to sleep until after three a.m. because all you can do is lie in bed and imagine different objects to pummel the director's head with.

Don't you love these sitcoms they hype up for a month or three on TV based on one joke that's in every single preview? Then once the show premieres, it's cancelled after two episodes. Isn't it great to hear the news that it's gone forever, and the writers are forced to find another star from a previously successful sitcom to build another sinking ship around?

Has someone ever asked you a question, and you answer it before he's done talking? Then, a second later, when he actually finishes asking the question, he waits for you to give another answer, as if he didn't hear you the first time? Pal, if I wasn't so intent on my response, I wouldn't have jumped in when I did.

Have you ever been cleaning up after a party that ran out of beer early? You'll be picking up cans the next morning and find some with only one sip gone from them. Who on the face of this earth would take just one sip of a beer? When I find you, you will drink this beer, no matter how long it takes me to hunt you down.

Restaurants that serve soda from a fountain behind the bar. You take one sip and then contemplate the fact that *you* paid *them* to drink it.

> Cursive is the stupidest—
> had to learn in school....
> long to write this as it—
> the same words in animal—
> be able to read what the

Why is it that every website I try to buy something from wants me to become a member? Say I'm shopping for gardening books for Aunt Wilma's birthday. I pick out the books at some website, click to buy them, and the site tells me I need to become a member to purchase something.

When will I ever need gardening books again? If Wilma wants more books, I'll come find you. What could you possibly need my name, address, email address, and daytime telephone number for? I hope you realize how much business you idiots lose for yourselves and create for the desktop calendar and book certificate industries from shoppers who reach the final step in your online purchasing process, and say the hell with this, and the hell with you.

Why are shopping malls kept so hot in the winter? The first week of October comes around, and FWWOOOOOOSHHHHHH. You stroll in with your winter jacket on, and twenty minutes later, you feel like you should've left two or three layers of skin at home.

> -fucking thing we ever
> ..It took me three times as
> would have taken to smear
> feces, and I would actually
> shit-stain words said;

You ever hear parents explain how their kid is really smart but "just doesn't test well"? Let me give them a test right now: What state do you live in? What country? What town? What street? What's your address? What's your phone number? How about your zip code? Well, you tested pretty well there, so what's the problem? There was no problem because you know these answers like the back of your hand. If you knew the material you were tested on in school that well, you'd be doing just fine. If your kid isn't doing as well as you'd like, either he's not trying hard enough, or maybe he isn't quite the Einstein you've been promoting.

Why do people spray-paint love confessions on highway overpasses? I wouldn't be very flattered seeing my name with a heart around it on I-80. Not to mention, how is this person going to know the graffiti is directed at her? If it just says I <3 Yolanda, how's the poor girl going to know it's for her unless you tell her? And if you do tell her, you're either going to be slapped by a hand or a restraining order, so why bother? There's no need to reinvent the wheel: flowers and a card for sex and a sandwich makes everyone a happy camper.

Why do they have to interview every player after every round of home run derby at the MLB All-Star Game?

"So, Frank, you seemed to get a hold of a few balls there."

"Yeah."

"Were you feeling a lot of pressure up there?"

"No."

"What was going through your head at the plate?"

"Well, that there were balls, and I should hit them."

"The very fearless Frank Pabon. Thank you, and back to the booth."

Scary movies with happy endings. The ending is what makes a scary movie, and a happy one always ruins it.

HEY DO YOU WANT ANOTHER BEER TOO?

UM, ACTUALLY I'LL HAVE A GREYGOOSE MARTINI, AND, TAMMY WHAT DO YOU WANT?

Movies that are built on a single one-liner. It goes without saying that this joke is tirelessly overplayed in every commercial, and effectively lowers the film's entertainment value to that of a beaver gnawing on your face for two hours.

When anyone explaining paintings in a museum includes the fact that a painting is "oil on canvas." It's always oil on canvas. In fact, why don't you keep quiet until it isn't oil on canvas? Just keep quiet then, too.

Fishing tournaments where officials stock a lake with fish, then award prize money for catching them.

Is anyone else confused by the Hess truck commercials at Christmas? I might be missing the point because the children look ecstatic to see a gas truck, but what exactly is the appeal of the thing?

In a football game when a player catches a kickoff and just kneels down in the end zone. Is that how you want to start the game? On your knees?

The Federal Reserve and its rate cuts. These people get together and move the rates up, and they move the rates down. Can't you come up with something a little more original? Why not feed a half dozen mountain lions nothing but mushrooms and Absinth for twenty-four hours, then let them loose on the Exchange floor? That ought to get things moving.

Have you ever been minding your own business somewhere, and you take out a breath mint, and someone else asks if he can have one? Ever notice how the person asking for the mint will never, at any point in his life, have mints to offer you?

Have you ever been on a plane when a movie's about to come on and the flight attendants offer to sell you headphones? One time, I asked why I had to pay $5 to watch the onboard movie. The attendant said, "If you didn't pay, it'd be like getting into the movies for free." Well, last time I checked, the theatres weren't charging $800 just to sit in their fucking seat.

Was there some amazing development in audio technology recently? Headphones seem awfully loud these days. I sit on a bus with some kid twenty feet away, and I can hear the song he's listening to! Why bother with the headphones? Or why not just stick your head in a jet engine for a half hour and get the whole hearing thing over with. It's reassuring to know most of these people will be deaf by the time they're thirty, when there'll be plenty of silence for both of us to enjoy then.

ATM arrows that appear to line up with the wrong buttons because of the angle of the screen. Why is it so hard to angle an ATM screen toward a normal person's eyes? You see many ten-year-olds making deposits these days?

When a professional photographer is taking a group photo and all the short people immediately head to the back and hope to stay there, but you have to waste time while the photographer barks at them to come forward and kneel down in front like the chumps they are.

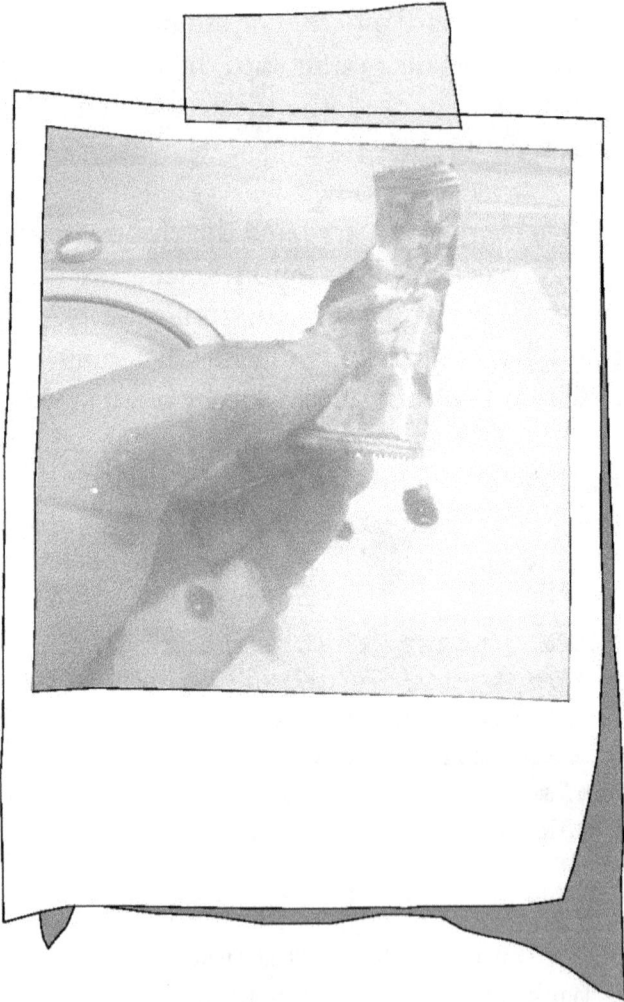

Punters on football teams with only one bar for a facemask.

Contests by soft drink or candy bar companies in which instead of telling you whether you won or not right away, they make you go to some stupid website and enter a code. Either tell me right there if I won, or that sucker's going in the trash quicker than a Kansas City Royals season.

Sinks designed so you have to continuously press down on one knob for water to come out. When you have to press down with one hand to get a stream of water, how can you wash the other hand? I've seen this before at fast food restaurants, right below a sign that says employees must wash hands before returning to work.

Can someone clear up why advertisements are shown before movies in theatres? A commercial advertisement is appropriate for things like TV or radio where paid admission is not available for generating revenue. Patrons are required to pay an admission fee to theatres often exceeding $12, and there is no necessary financial reason to play Coca-Cola or luxury car ads in a theatre. In other words, get your shit off the screen because I was neutral to begin with, but now feel more inclined to burn down your dealership and celebrate with a Pepsi.

In Scrabble, when someone wastes a triple word score on a word like "AT" or "COW."

When I'm forced to use a pen that's so low on ink I have to write each letter two or three times to be able to see it. It's especially annoying when it's the pen a bank provides to fill out deposit slips. You know, you guys are the ones who are going to have to decipher the chicken scratch I carve into this thing. I'd think you'd at least want to provide a writing utensil less than ten years old that wasn't pulled from the seat crack of a Buick.

Limited-time offers at fast food restaurants. Why do they invent a delicious form of fast food and offer it for only a limited time? People like me get hooked on these things and then get pissed off when you stop serving them. I don't even try special promotions anymore just for that reason.

The flippant small talk exchanged between newscasters on TV. First, one of them will make an oh-so-hilarious remark. Then someone else will top that remark with a comeback. Then the weatherman will chime in with a punch line, and everyone will be rolling on the floor. These dialogues are usually based on athletic ability or New Year's resolutions and are very hard to watch without directing a sharp object at your wrist.

When you have a cold and you blow your nose so many times that the tissues start to feel like sandpaper.

Have you ever had to listen to people who can't identify colors correctly? You'll see a pond full of orange goldfish, and they'll say, "Look at all the red fish!" Or you'll hear a referee during a soccer game award the ball to the "blue" team when it's clearly purple. Then there's the other type who are too good for normal colors. They'll point out that the traffic light is "amber," not yellow. Or they'll use words like magenta, pastel, and ochre. The word purple exists, too, for those of you who insist on over-glorifying the term "violet." Using language as a smokescreen to sound sophisticated is about as difficult to recognize as an Escalade coming through your living room wall.

Televised sporting events where the score isn't continuously shown on the screen.

People say dying in your sleep is the best way to go. I beg to differ. After a nightmare, people like to wake up safe in their beds. Imagine having a nightmare and waking up in hell.

Have you ever been on a road you've driven on for years, and you notice a new empty lot? So you get really upset and think about how the open space is an eyesore, and it's a shame that they changed the local scenery, and they tore down a beautiful old house. Then you think really hard and can't quite remember what was there, or if there was anything at all.

In chess when two players stare at the board for ten minutes while each thinks it's the other's turn.

When you go out of your way to be a nice person and give someone a ride in your car, and he gets out and leaves a coffee cup, soda can, sandwich wrapper, or an empty bag of chips behind for you to clean up.

When you balance your checkbook and the numbers are off by more than a dollar, because a dollar is too much to ignore. If it was 45 or 82 cents, so what? Feed it to the birds. But once it crosses that three-digit threshold, it burrows into your psyche, and you spend countless commercial breaks during AMC's Saturday afternoon movie adding and re-adding numbers. When you've finally determined that math itself has failed, given the circumstances, you start rationalizing actions that would normally fall into a moral grey zone. Actions like slapping a child to the ground and taking her lunch money to even the ledger.

When you're stuck in traffic in the summer with your left arm hanging out the window, and you show up where you're going with the only thing that's worse than a farmer's tan: a trucker's tan.

When you're speaking with a guy who talks so damn slow that you can already tell what he's going to say after two words, and you just want to spit out the rest of the sentence for him.

Fishermen who hang out on golf courses. There are places for you to be, and this isn't one of them. Be gone.

Why are there so many movies about male characters dressing up like women to get away with something? It's a cheap gag for given laughs, but the idea itself is so overused it's just becoming boring.

When you really need to wake up for something in the morning, but you actually set your alarm for 7:30 p.m. like the winner you are.

Have you ever heard health "experts" tell you to drink eight glasses of water a day to stay healthy? I tried that one time and spent more time pissing than I did sleeping the night before.

Have you ever seen commercials explaining why it's important to update the aesthetics of money in order to thwart counterfeiters? Why is this on TV? I don't care what money looks like. I don't even care if someone uses counterfeit money on me, as long as the next guy will take it, too. It's like these people are using our tax dollars to produce commercials to convince us that their job is necessary in the first place

Besides, does anyone realistically have a say in the whole thing anyway? What if they wanted to color all money red, starting next week? They could decide to put the Unabomber on the nickel, and what could you do? Write a letter? That's what the Unabomber did, and look where it got him. OK, maybe my Xerox scam just went to shit, and I'm a little bitter.

Anyone who identifies the breed or cross-breed of every dog that walks past. There are big dogs, there are little dogs, and there are dogs that won't shut the hell up, and that's about it.

Jeans pockets that are so tight you can't pull your hand out of them without drawing blood.

Don't you hate it when you're watching a game show on TV, and they stop the game to talk to contestants about their personal lives? Jeopardy, Deal or No Deal, Wheel of Fortune, they all do it. Let me speak on behalf of everyone who's ever watched television: we don't care who you are, where you're from, how many children you have, or what you do for a living. Really, we don't.

Two consecutive traffic lights on a road, less than one hundred yards apart, that are perfectly out of sync.

Anyone who knocks on wood, and when you look into his eyes, you see that he really means it.

Ever been to a restaurant where the waitress is taking your order and asks what kind of dressing you'd like on your salad? You tell her you're not hungry enough for a salad, and she gives the standard waitress response:

"But it comes with your meal."
I don't care, I don't want it.
"But it comes with your meal."
If you bring it out, it's going to sit untouched on the table in front of me. I'll still pay for it. Just leave it there for someone else.
"But it comes with your meal."
"Under no circumstances would I like a striptease."
"But it comes with your . . ."

When you bite into a hard taco, the bottom crumbles, and everything falls out.

Have you ever met someone who tries to give you directions by drawing maps in the air with his fingers? He'll say, "Okay, this is the parking lot." And he'll make a box in the air. "Now this is Elm Street, and over here's Main." And he'll start waving his hands through the air in directions with no relevance at all to where anything else is. "So you know how to just go up this way and turn here . . ." And you have no clue what the bastard's trying to say so you just strap him into the front seat and start driving.

When radio show hosts let prank calls go too long, to the point where the person asks if it's a prank.

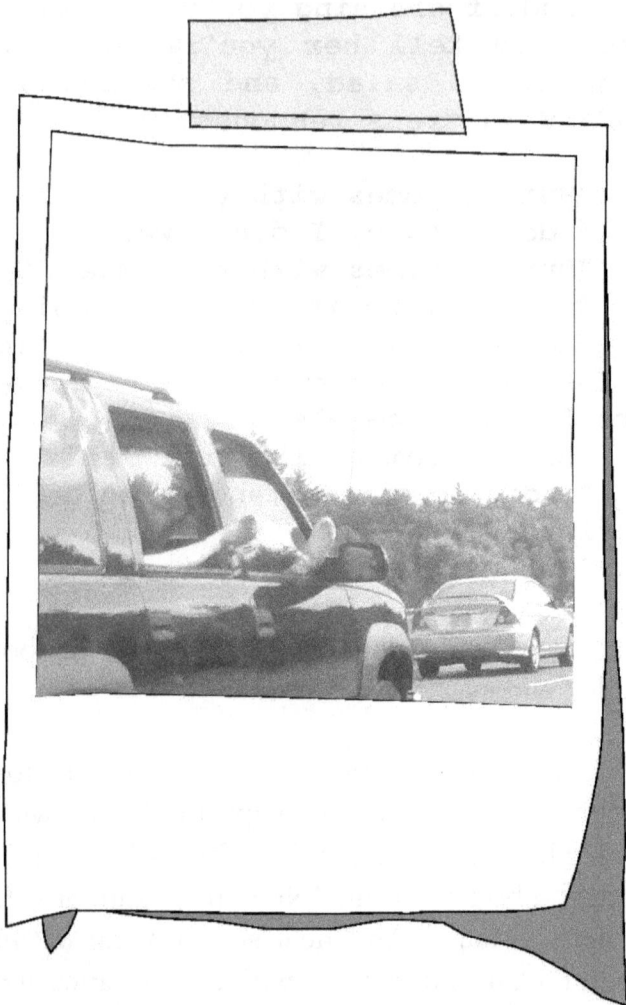

I can't tell you how much you've enhanced the experience of this six hour drive by displaying the fungal petri dish that is afixed to the end of your leg. Thank you.

Have you ever boarded a packed elevator in a tall building, and the elevator stops at the second or third floor, and someone toward the back wants to get off? The term "kiss my ass" takes on more of a literal meaning than usual in this scenario.

Did you ever watch *The Price Is Right* and see some of those contestants who had no confidence? All of them look out to the audience for help from people who are shouting and holding up fingers like they know any better. I wonder what ran through Bob Barker's head during these moments he must have experienced thousands of times over the years: probably all the twisted ways you really could spay or neuter a house pet.

At amusement parks when you climb into a roller-coaster car, pull down the harness, and wait for the attendant to walk past and check it. Ever notice how they don't always check too hard? They just sort of press down with a finger or two? I mean, my life's at stake here, and you're not even going to give it a good shake? It sure looks like a few of the kids working there wouldn't hesitate shaking me down in the parking lot.

Have you ever seen a guest on a talk show who just doesn't know when to shut up? You'll be watching Leno or Letterman, some moron comes out, and the host might be able to say, "So how are you?" before the person just starts rambling off stories and telling jokes. Then, at the end, the person will try to plug his awful movie with a clip, and the host will go to a commercial instead. It's a feeling of satisfaction on par with passing someone on the right who's going fifty-five in a passing lane, then cutting him off just to make a point.

At a hockey game when Zambonies are circling the rink and one of them misses a sliver of ice.

People who try to bring strollers on escalators with the kids sitting in them.

People at the beach who leave untouched globs of sunscreen on their noses.

Why does every movie feel the need to make a trilogy? Just because the original *Star Wars* did well, now every Joe with a script wants to go for it. *Jurassic Park*, *Home Alone*, *Dumb and Dumber*, *The Little Mermaid 3: Ariel Whores Herself in Cancun*. Where does it end?

When you take a piss outside somewhere where there's a slope slanting back toward your feet. It's usually during a long, beer-induced piss, too, so you have to shuffle your feet around in a little dance to avoid the back-flow.

When you ring the doorbell at someone's house and a bunch of dogs start barking and running around.

People who sleep on the street to buy the latest new version of a stupid new technological gadget, then act like they won the lottery when they buy it. The thing is going to be obsolete in two months so who cares?

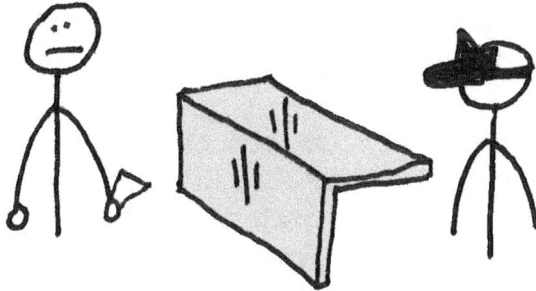

So Do You Serve Fecal Sandwiches or Are You the only piece of shit in here right now?

Bagel shops that still put half a pound of cream cheese on a bagel even when you ask specifically for a little.

When you're having your hair cut, and the barber goes to trim your hair with the electric clippers, and the battery is always dead.

When sports journalists refer to an event as the "game of the century," then use the same term five years later.

Parents who encourage the celebration of their child's half-birthday.

Can't they do something about bench-clearing brawls in baseball? Why not have a sniper in the outfield ready to take out anyone who leaves the bench? Now there's a good pick-off play.

Why do professional sports leagues even bother handing out suspensions? If they're going to suspend a player, there should be no appeals. Whenever a suspension is given, even if it's a single game, the player appeals it. While the appeal is pending, the player can continue playing until the penalty is reconsidered.

For fuck's sake, it's a two-game suspension from playing baseball, not twenty-five to life. You're basically told you can't go down to the park and play because your mom grounded you for the weekend. Does it make sense for Timmy to continue playing after filing an appeal with his father about the decision? Shut up and sit on the bench. You wouldn't have been the topic for suspension in the first place if you'd used your head.

The way a vending machine looks like it still doesn't give a shit after you scream and hit it for taking your money.

Animal enthusiasts who go through the woods to find animal dung just to look through it to see what the animal ate. There's a reason you don't get laid.

Anyone who tells me I can't have my cake and eat it, too. What the hell else would I do with my cake?

Soccer players faking fouls and collapsing on the field like they've been shot. For those who would claim that Americans aren't sophisticated enough to appreciate the "beautiful" game, it's this kind of crap that keeps people here from taking the sport seriously. Every three minutes, one of these guys is writhing on the ground because someone pulled on his jersey. I don't see the snipers who are taking them out, but let me know if you do, and I'll help them put these players out of all the misery they appear to be in.

When some dick cop on TV is about to arrest someone, but asks that person if he has any drugs or weapons he wants to tell the officer about. Then if the person tells the cop he does, he gets charged just the same as if he'd stayed silent and made the cop search his anus. I say let the two assholes meet and get to know each other.

When old people give you dirty looks for trying to pass them in grocery store aisles.

Joggers who run in place at traffic lights.

Couples who walk down the street with their hands in each other's back pockets. What happened to just holding hands? If you're going to go that far, why not just stick your hands down each other's pants? Grab a little flesh. Make it interesting for the rest of us.

Anyone who actually knows all the words to that song people sing at midnight on New Year's, and makes it a point to sing them loudly so everyone can hear.

Sports fans who yell at college athletes for underperforming. These pasty, balding, overweight clowns sit in the stands and bark at college athletes who aren't receiving a dime for the millions they're bringing into their respective schools. As if, at any point in their lives, these hecklers could do anything remotely as athletic as the players on the court. Why don't you slip on your home whites there, tubby, and show us how it's done?

I get tired of news stations with common-interest stories about people whose ancestors came from other countries who have lived in America their whole lives and want to "find their identities." They'll talk about how this person is confused about their background so the person takes a trip to the country of his heritage, walks around, talks to crusty ninety-eight-year-old shop owners about how his great-grandfather was a carpenter *AND* a stable hand . . . Zzzz. You know? If it makes them happy, that's great. But does it have to go on right before the weekend forecast on the ten o'clock news?

When people insist on using contrived, artifical devices to make themselves feel better without actually changing anything of substance. For instance, some people use the term "BCE" instead of "BC." They say it's the politically correct choice, since BC stands for "Before Christ" and BCE stands for "Before the Common Era." Obviously, this was derived out of fear that people who aren't Christian would be offended by the term "Before Christ." What I don't understand is that if you're going to go through the trouble and the hoopla of renaming a well-known, well-established system, why not come up with numbering based on a different, non-religious event as well?

It seems like simply using a different label to refer to the years since Christ was guessed to have been born would almost be more insulting to non-Christians than having to say, "Before Christ." It sounds kind of like, "We don't care enough to entirely recalibrate how time is measured in the modern world, so we'll just rename what we have and hope that's enough to keep you quiet, so we can avoid dealing with the issue and give ourselves a pat on the back."

To me, it would be like making the effort not to call the new Meadowlands Stadium "Giants Stadium" out of consideration for Jets fans but then leaving the whole place painted blue with "GIANTS" written in each end zone for every game. I say either completely redo the whole thing, just be honest and leave the terms the way they are, or get rid of the stupid terms altogether. Why don't we just officially convert to the existing calendar of Super Bowl years, and we'll refer to anything before that as, "Before Commercial Excruciation"?

Stories on the news about a beached whale or a whale caught in fishing nets. I'll stop there because you've already stopped paying attention.

Unfunny comedy show hosts can really ruin an evening. Especially right after a good comedian's been on, and the host strolls back on the stage as if the audience was laughing at him or her and just plain ruins the mood with his or her dumb jokes. The worst is when the host doesn't keep it crisp and get on to the next performer, but just sort of hangs around like a legitimate attraction.

When you get out of the shower but the weather's so hot that you're covered in sweat before you finish drying, and you never actually experience the feeling of being dry.

Guys who say they "hate to lose" like it's some unique personal trait. Some hormone-injected crotch of a professional athlete will tell a reporter, "I just personally hate to lose so I hope this never happens again." Well, that's interesting. It's certainly a different perspective from all the guys I know who hate to win. Thanks for that intellectual breath of fresh air.

When you're looking for something specific on a bunch of different websites, and you're spending five or ten seconds on each site. Then occasionally you run into sites where you have to stop and wait thirty seconds for animation to load, or music will play the whole time, or a message says I can't see any graphics because I need to download a Flash 11 plug-in player, and do I want to download it now, and it may require restarting my computer, and can I just see your fucking website?

When tips are included in a bill. The purpose of a tip is to reward good service, so it kind of defeats the whole purpose when you eliminate the motivation behind earning it.

People who leave drinks on pool table railings.

What the hell am
I supposed to do,
drive the other way
in reverse?

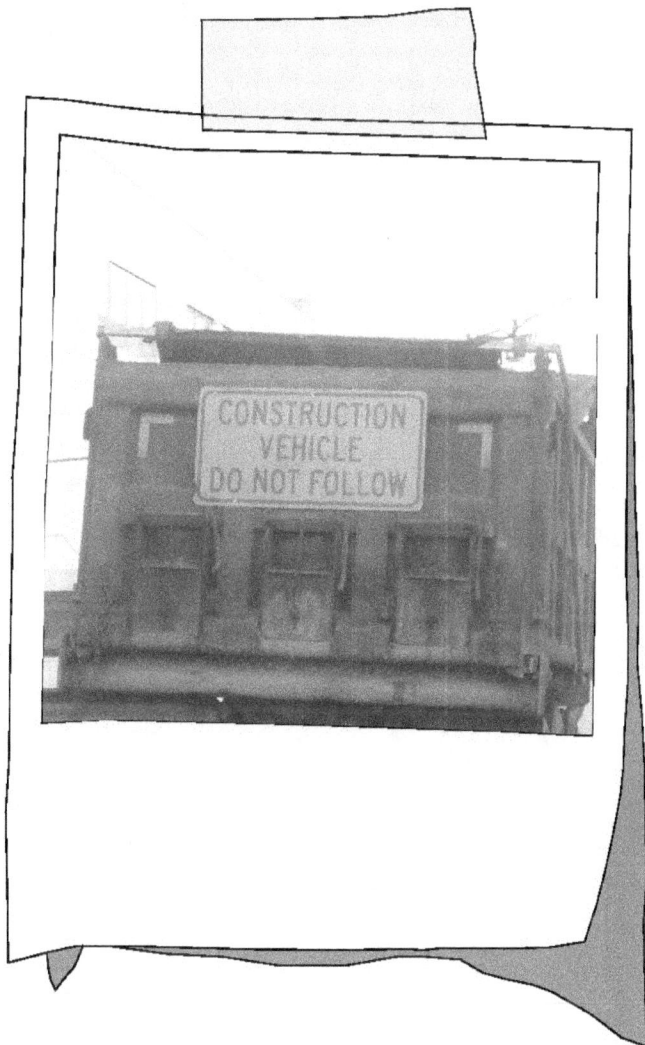

When you're having your blood pressure checked, doesn't it seem like they just sort of look at the gauge and pick a number? The nurse squeezes the pump a couple of times, waits a few seconds, watches the needle float around, and spits out something like "129." If you're going to make up numbers, why not spice things up with a roulette wheel, and let patients bet on their blood pressure? Someone in healthcare is going to end up with that money one way or another, so why not have a little fun with it? You could even let patients double down on their co-payments to kick things off on the way in. Yes, I would love an informative letter explaining the precise methods used to check blood pressure, and I'm looking forward to it.

When you order something at Starbucks and the people working there correct your order. You ask for a caramel cappuccino with whipped cream and they'll shoot back, "The Star Dust Cappu-Caramel Whipped Dream?" Actually, just give me a pot of black coffee. Make sure it's extra hot, too, because it's going right in your face.

When you're watching a game on TV and the people broadcasting it are trying to balance airtime between the game itself and an interview with someone standing on the sidelines or sitting in the stands. These aren't quick interviews, either. They drag on and on, and it's usually with someone no one cares about, like some actor or politician. Don't you hate it when they miss a play because they're showing this person's face instead of the game and then they try to switch back, but it's too late? So let's review this point just in case you didn't get the message: NO ONE WANTS TO LISTEN TO

INTERVIEWS ON THE SIDELINES, IN THE STANDS, OR IN THE ANNOUNCERS' BOOTH WITH *ANYONE* . . . I'D RATHER STAPLE MY SCROTUM TO THE SIDE OF A MOVING VEHICLE THAN SIT THROUGH ONE OF THESE. PLEASE SHOW ONLY THE GAME ITSELF, BECAUSE, BELIEVE IT OR NOT, THAT'S WHY PEOPLE ARE WATCHING YOUR STATION AT THIS MOMENT: TO NOT FEEL OBLIGED TO ENGAGE THEIR ATTENTION IN WATCHING SEVERAL FORCED, AWKWARD CONVERSATIONS.

When did leaving a message on a cell phone become more of a hassle than bailing a friend out of jail? It used to be a recording and a beep. Now it's a recording and "If you would like to send a text message to appear on the phone of the person you are calling, press six now. To page the person you are calling, press five now. To hear Chewbacca scream in frustration, press eight now. At the sound of the tone, you may record your message. When you are finished recording, you may hang up or jerk off to the sound of the dial tone . . ."

"News coverage" of a local heat wave. What can you tell me that I don't already know?

When you're checking out at a store, and the first thing the clerk does is ask for your phone number. How many real numbers do you think you get on an average day? I mean really, if you're going to be that upfront about what a pain in the ass you're willing to be to your customers, why not just make them walk through a swarm of hornets as they leave and get a good laugh, too?

When you hand cashiers money, why do they announce how much you've just given them?

"Out of ten."

That's observant, but why are you saying this? Is it a question? Then pose it as a question.

"Out of ten?"

Well, in that case, no. Here're a couple of $100 bills. Let's make it out of $510, okay? Could I get mostly singles back, too? I'm headed to a gentlemen's club now, and you know how bartenders get when you ask them for change.

Straw dispensers at fast food restaurants where the straws are already taken out of the wrappers. It's not an inconvenience for me to take off a wrapper. In fact, they're actually fun to shoot at people. More importantly, though, I don't know what the hell's been touching that straw before it gets near my lips. For all I know, Ronald McDonald and Grimace broke in last night and used that straw to snort lines off a hooker's chest in the ball pit. On that thought, you might also want to poke around the ball pit with a mop before letting any kids in.

When someone giving a talk or a lecture constantly pesters members of the audience with "yes" or "no" questions to be answered by a show of hands. Just finish your little talk and let people voice their opinions at the Q and A session afterward. At that point, I can exercise my opinion that it's time to be somewhere else.

Popcorn-flavored jelly beans.

When you get a refund or rebate from a big company for $3 or $4 in the mail, and it comes in the form of a check.

Anyone who refers to a sport as a "game of inches," like it's something special. What sport isn't?

When you're buying something online and they tell you not to hit the "submit order" button more than once because it will charge your card twice. So you hit the submit button, nothing happens, and after a few seconds, a box appears that says Internet Explorer has an error and needs to shut down. Well, did the order go through or not?

Why do some people insist on putting so much time, effort, and money into accessorizing piece-of-shit cars? Why don't they just save up some money and buy a respectable car? I saw a minivan with rims blasting a sound system as it passed my house once. Getting pumped for soccer practice?

When you put a DVD into a player, and it automatically starts playing. Do you ever start watching a DVD from the second you put it in? Of course not. You want to go get a sandwich and a drink, make a call, and go to the bathroom. Then you want to sit down, get comfortable, and maybe even catch the weather before you start the movie. But when you finally turn it on, you always have to hit "stop," go back to the main menu, and play again because it's already seven minutes into the show.

People who walk their dogs off leashes in cemeteries. All dogs go to heaven, except if they shit on a headstone.

Saturday Night Live hasn't been good since the 90s.

When you have your hand stamped at a bar and the next day you have to go to work, but you can't get the stupid ink to wash off.

Blues Brothers impersonators who take themselves more seriously than a rent-a-clown.

Have you ever been at a basketball game when they have some on-court competition at halftime with people from the stands? Are the contestants you watch as terrible as the ones I see? The contest will be to shoot a lay-up, foul shot, three-pointer, and half-court shot in thirty seconds, and they'll bring out some four-and-a-half-foot Aunt Edna and tell everyone to cheer their hearts out while she's under-handing air balls from three feet away. This is entertainment? Why not just bring the twelve drunkest fans you can find out on the court, fence them in, and have some kid mow them down with the T-shirt cannon for ten minutes instead?

Don't you wish some nights they'd just cancel the news? You know, say at the start, "Nothing worth reporting today." Then watch the anchors down a bottle of gin and play adult Pictionary on the weatherman's blue screen for a half hour.

Why do people worry about bringing home unsolicited gifts for friends while they're on vacation? It's your vacation, why should you spend the whole time worried about other people? If they want something from Acapulco, tell them to hop on a plane and get it themselves, the inconsiderate pricks. You have to worry about waking up in time for your two o'clock nap.

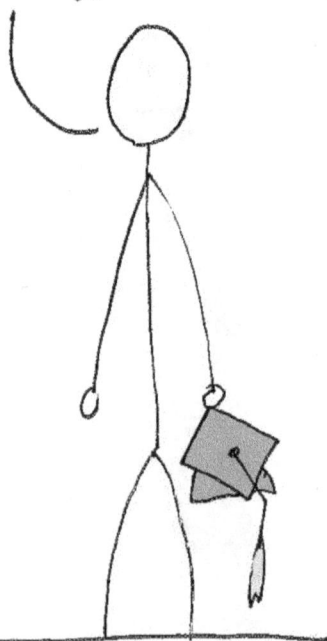

People who openly admit to watching the Super Bowl just for the commercials. Is it that much to ask you to sit down and watch one game a year? I don't know what you like to tell yourself in terms of your sophistication, but you're not impressing anyone.

The people who criticize the use of stereotypes are usually the ones who use them the most.

When you give a bum some change, and he follows you asking for more. He'll jump in the street and hail a cab for you, or hold open a door to a restaurant, all the while asking for a dollar. If you get some coins, it's called being a bum. If you get some dollars, it's called having a job.

People who blatantly pick their noses in public and think it's less offensive because they put a Kleenex over their fingers. Why can't you do this in private? Everyone picks his nose at some point, but that's like watching you have sex with a sheet over your head in the food court at the mall. Who are you kidding?

Have you ever taken a piss in a public restroom and the only other guy in there is pissing, too, but he's breathing really deeply with every push like he's lifting weights? It's very disconcerting to be stuck in this situation and helpless to leave for thirty or forty seconds.

When you're sitting in a bathroom stall by yourself and some guy walks in, thinks he has the place to himself, and leaks mustard shells into the toilet next to you. Then he'll walk out, go on with his life, and leave you with an unexpected sentence to the gas chamber.

When you hold on to things like old action figures or three hundred *National Geographic* magazines for twenty-five years thinking they'll be worth something some day. Then you go on eBay and see everything you collected going for a buck fifty, total.

When you get a bill or solicitation in the mail from a credit card company and they send you a few checks with your name and information printed on them to use at your convenience. Other than having my intelligence offended by the company thinking I'm stupid enough to go on a spending spree with those, isn't it just a little obnoxious that not only do I have to throw out junk mail but also have to cut up the stupid checks too so no one else can use them?

Doctors who try to predict children's heights. They're always wrong when it comes to who's going to be short and tall. Listen, bud, first learn how to write better than the kid you're measuring, and then you can whip out your crystal ball.

When you're with a tour group walking through some old house or museum, and after about half the people file into a room, one person just stops, stands in the doorway, and blocks everyone else. They do bag checks at the front door, and apparently lobotomies, too. Stop staring at the painting on the ceiling and move your ass into the damn room. I know you came on the short tour bus, but let's not ruin everyone's day.

HOWDY YA'LL!

I'M A SELF-PROCLAIMED "DALLAS COWBOYS FAN"! I RESIDE IN YOUR LOCAL COMMUNITY AND NEVER RESIST THE CHANCE TO LET YOU KNOW WHEN AMERICA'S TEAM PULLS OUT A BIG WIN! EVEN THOUGH THE ONLY TIME I'VE BEEN TO TEXAS WAS ON A ONE-HOUR LAYOVER, MY KNOWLEDGE OF LIFE THERE IS BASED EXCLUSIVELY ON RERUNS OF KING OF THE HILL, AND THERE'S AT LEAST A 6 OUT OF 10 CHANCE THAT I COULDN'T NAME THAT STATE'S CAPITAL WITHOUT CONSULTING GOOGLE...

GO 'BOYYYS!

HEEE HAAA!

Round-shaped toilet seats may look perfectly acceptable to the female eye, but when it comes to sitting down for men, there's a significant problem. Or maybe a small one, it depends on the guy.

People who talk to golf balls mid-flight as if the ball will change its mind about where it's going.

Bars that aren't filled to capacity but still keep people waiting in line out on the street. You think your place will look more popular if you keep a healthy line out front? Well, it's not hard to see past the smoke and mirrors when someone looks inside and sees there's enough open space for three sex offenders and an elementary school to coexist within legal limits inside.

When you're going through customs after coming home from another country and the customs agent is a real asshole, but you know you can't say anything because he holds the power to keep your ass out of the country.

I've had it with postcards. Everyone says, "Send me a postcard!" How 'bout I just come home and tell you about my trip? I'll get there before the postcard would anyway.

Open-faced sandwiches. If it's open-faced, it's not a sandwich. It's an inconvenience.

When you're sitting in the aisle seat on an airplane and every time someone in the row behind you gets up or sits down, he pulls back on the corner of your headrest and lets it snap forward.

When a bunch of people push their way on to a subway car or an elevator before everyone else who wants to has gotten off first.

Catholics who say that for Lent they won't give up anything, but they'll just be a lot nicer to people. That's not the point. Jesus went into the desert for forty days to sacrifice comfort and fight temptation, not to be nice to scorpions. The bottom line is sacrifice, not friendliness. Just so you know, you can't always find an excuse not to diet.

When some self-glorifying car company runs advertisements about the return of the company's annual sale, as if I'm supposed to care. No one buys a new car every year, and if people do, it won't be from you every time. So why do you tell people not to miss "Toyotathon '11" like they've attended the last ten Toyotathons? It's not a concert. No one's going to wear T-shirts for Toyotathon '92 and be proud of it. People are going to buy a car when they need one, not when you put up a banner and balloons. Please cease the needless hype.

When people shut the door to a bathroom even if no one's using it. For example, at a party, you'll be standing outside the bathroom for five minutes before you finally knock and realize no one's even in there!

So you were willing
to drive your kids
from the house to the
end of the driveway,
but that's where the
line gets drawn, huh?

People who lean on their horns when there's a traffic jam in an underground parking garage. You know your horn gets a lot fucking LOUDER when you're in a small, enclosed space.

On the show *Extreme Home Makeover* when they do a theme in a kid's room based on something the kid is obsessed with like pixies, or shellfish, or loan sharking, and they fit the place with tens of thousands of dollars worth of shit. What happens when the kid's sick of that fad in six months and has moved on to banshees, or water polo, or Jack Daniels, or whatever he's into next?

Why do video-game makers assume that the more realistic they can make a game, the better it will be? Nothing's left to the imagination when you have every player, his home, away, and alternate jerseys, exact arena layouts, shooting percentages, towel-lengths, and erectile dysfunction frequencies.

You know what I liked? Ice Hockey for the original Nintendo. Not Wayne Gretzky's NHL 3D All-Star Challenge 2012, just plain Ice Hockey. The only difference between the players was that some were fat and some were skinny. It was pure gaming talent, not accumulated yearly statistics that made the saves, shot the pucks, and scored the goals on their own.

When a football team is lining up quickly so the quarterback can spike the ball to stop the clock, and the referee throws a flag because someone wasn't set. Just let them spike the damn ball.

Have you ever gone to the beach and had to put on a lot of sunscreen? You're aware you should also put some on your back, but you're too lazy to get someone else to do it, so you just reach around and put on as much as you can. Then when you take a shower in the afternoon your back feels burnt, so you look in the mirror and see all the places where your fingers reached as far as they could with the lotion. They're called "asshole marks," and their name is derived from the bearer.

I can't stand it when I say that I'm going shopping on December 20th, and someone gives me a nudge and a wink about "last-minute shopping." Last-minute shopping takes place after six p.m. on Christmas Eve.

Why are fortune cookies more like statements than fortunes now? "Your heart is the most sensitive part of your body." So where's the fortune? What happened to "By the look of that gut, I'd say your future has about five or six more cookies in it"?

Have you ever had to deal with one of these cement-heads on the highway who drives really slowly, so you go to pass him and he speeds up then so you can't get by? The car usually has New York plates on it, and unless he's receiving road head, I have no sympathy for his actions.

What happened to simple fruit juice flavors? What's the need for "Cran-Apple-Dingleberry Splash?"

Restaurants that give you glasses of water so small you finish the whole thing in two gulps and end up asking the waiter for five or six refills throughout the meal.

Arrogant foreigner cashiers who don't know what they're doing, but still give their customers attitude. If you're learning to speak English, that's fine, I'll speak slowly and give you a break. What gets to me is when no one can understand what you're saying because you're talking a thousand miles an hour, then you act annoyed with a customer who's politely trying to work with you.

When I say on three distinct occasions that I don't want a Heath Bar Blizzard, I want a Peanut Butter Cup Blizzard, and I still get a Heath Bar Blizzard, any sensible employee would apologize and rectify the situation. So before you tell me off as an incompetent consumer and shoot me a dirty look, at least learn what the phrase "service with a smile" means. Because that's what keeps our service industry a notch above the rest:

our ability to make people think we care at all about the quality of a total stranger's ice cream.

People who cover their luggage with Saran Wrap.

AND THE ACTUAL RETAIL PRICE IS...

$1300 $1301

When you come to a stop at an intersection and you need to lean forward to look both ways, but your seatbelt locks, and you can't lean forward to see anything.

Who's responsible for the "speed patrolled by aircraft" signs on highways? You know, it was one thing to put out electronic signs that told me how fast I was going, because that had me feeling guilty for about half a second, but don't think I'm an idiot. There is no airplane, and even if there is, it's never going to be used unless the governor's stopping by for a photo-op. Between fuel, pilot's fees, and downright impracticality, it would cost entirely too much to operate. I may drive over the speed limit, but that doesn't mean I drive too fast.

What's all this nonsense about tracking systems in cars? People say they want to feel safe knowing someone will call an ambulance when the airbags go off, or that a guidance system will tell them where to go, or that a locator will tell police where to find the car if it's stolen.

First of all, if you're in an accident, either it's your time to go or it's not, so let the cards fall where they may. Secondly, if you don't know where you're going, buy a fucking map. And, finally, the last thing I need is for the authorities to know where I am at any point. Talk about violating civil liberties. Forget about wiretaps, what if I'm the one stealing the car? How's GPS going to help me then?

How about people who convey news of a sad event while giggling and smiling? It's a tough subject for them to discuss, so they try to disguise their grief by sounding happy.

"So when I was like thirteen, I was in a boat, and like a shark dove on board and ate my sisters and like half of my dad, and it was like, awful, so that wasn't very good, you know? Hee hee hee."

If you're going to talk about something bad, look like it. I can deal with someone crying for a few minutes, but a person who giggles when he talks about his dog chasing a tennis ball into a wood chipper is just disturbing.

When are golfers going to realize that a bigger driver doesn't mean better golf? Who cares if the ball goes three hundred yards if you can't hit it straight? For a lot of people, it just means a longer walk into the woods. Just remember, $500 and fifteen extra yards doesn't mean a whole lot when you still three-putt every hole.

When you're watching a big championship game on TV and the game ends and you have to listen to all the players and coaches drone on about how they've worked so hard and been through so much adversity, and overcome so many things. So what? There's a waffle eating contest three channels up.

I can't stand when they have to come up with some stupid reason in a movie to explain how a superhero or a villain transformed from a normal human being into what he or she is now. In the old *Batman* TV show, there were just the Joker, the Penguin, and the Riddler, with no questions asked. Now we have to spend a quarter of the stupid movie, time that could be spent on shooting and killing, to walk through just how Poison Ivy went from being a woman to a rash.

When I ask people from California where they live and they give me the name of a county. Like I'm supposed to have a clue where San Chalupa County is. If I were from Kansas, I wouldn't tell someone I was from Sheep County. I'd say I live an hour east of Wichita or two hours west of Kansas City. Only in California do you run across the pretentiousness of people expecting everyone to know offhand where their counties are located in relation to LA, the ocean, or anywhere else within fifty yards they can find an excuse to drive to.

THE LEAGUE WHERE A TRAVELING VIOLATION HASN'T BEEN CALLED SINCE 1972!...

...A LEAGUE WHERE NO ONE EVEN RUNS BACK DOWN THE COURT... WHEN THEY'RE ON OFFENSE!!....

BUMS

... AND NO ONE PLAYS DEFENSE, BECAUSE EVERY PLAYER REALIZED THAT IT'S EASIER TO JUST LET THE OTHER TEAM SCORE IN ORDER TO GET THE BALL BACK!

THAT'S WHY THE SCORE BETWEEN TWO MEDIOCRE TEAMS FROM OBSCURE CITIES THAT AREN'T HOME TO ANY OTHER PROFESSIONAL SPORTS TEAM IS...

HOME Q AWAY
186 2 152

AND THE MOST AMUSING THING TO WATCH ON THE COURT IS SOME RECENTLY-PAROLED SEX OFFENDER DRESSED AS A HAIRY MUPPET BASTARD CHILD WITH A T-SHIRT GUN AND A FOAM SCHLONG THAT HE OPENLY GROPES IN FRONT OF CHILDREN..

00

XXX

When you pay for gas with a credit card, but the machine at the pump is out of paper, and it tells you to see the cashier for a receipt. Obviously, I don't care enough to walk inside, but if I did though, I'd go inside, retrieve my receipt, and slit the cashier's eyelids off with it, so next time he doesn't have any trouble seeing that the receipt roll has never, ever been replaced since the station first opened.

When you're visiting a place where people get angry if you walk on the grass. Grass was meant to be walked on, and if you can't get over that, just pave your stupid lawn and at least then I can park closer.

When a pack of gum clearly states on the package the cost is 25 cents, but the store charges you 75 cents.

When a TV commercial tells you a product normally would cost you $400, but during this one-time offer, it can be yours for two easy payments of $37.95! Who says it's normally sold at $400? It's your stupid product to begin with; it's not like anyone else is selling it. I know you're still ripping me off by charging $76 so the fact you'd even joke about $400 earns an instant channel change.

What's all this shit on TV about horseracing? Have you ever seen one of these pre-game shows they have for the Preakness or the Belmont? God forbid there's a horse going for the Triple Crown. They must hire a scriptwriter for these hyped-up pageants because for a while I couldn't tell if I was watching ESPN on a Saturday afternoon or *Seabiscuit*. They'll go on for hours about some stupid horse that never had a chance and some no-name jockey who broke all his teeth and was snapped in two back in 1988 but still insists on riding. Then they'll do montages on the trainer and the owner until you can't help but shed a tear and actually get excited for the race. Then they have the race, it's over in a minute and a half, and the horse they profiled finishes sixth.

You know what they should do? They should follow people who bet money on the race, because they're the only ones who ultimately care. Profile some washed-up toll booth attendant who sold two illegitimate children and his kidney so he could bet $1,000 on the horse Morning Wood. Then watch the agony as he loses all his money and follow him home. There's actually potential for a post-game show with this. Get the guy all boozed up beforehand, too, and during the race hand him a baseball bat and some hand grenades. Now that's horseracing.

When you order take-out food at a restaurant, go inside to pick it up, pay with a credit card, and the receipt has a space for "tip" on it. What for? Making my food? That's called the bill, asshole. You think I just throw tips around to anyone I do business with? Walk me home, hold the door, throw in a happy ending, and maybe I'll reconsider.

Any "No U-Turn" sign. Creative driving should never be inhibited in any way.

When someone talking to a news camera clearly has his or her eyes on the Teleprompter and not the camera.

HI, I'M SOME BRAINLESS ANIMAL-LOVER ON TV IN SOME REMOTE WILDERNESS OR MAYBE EVEN SOME EXOTIC PET OWNER HERE TO PROVE SOME GOD-KNOWS-WHAT POINT ABOUT SOME KIND OF FEROCIOUS BEAST...

I'M GOING TO SLOWLY MAKE THIS SAVAGE PREDATOR TRUST ME AND MY PRESENCE BY SPENDING INORDINATE AMOUNTS OF TIME IN THE FIELD OR SOME CAGE SLOWLY CREEPING CLOSER...

GENERIC CARNIVORE

I WANT TO CARESS AND TREAT THIS ANIMAL LIKE A DAMN HOUSE PET AND TRY TO CONVINCE YOU THAT THIS IS REALLY A MISUNDERSTOOD CREATURE, EVEN THOUGH IT COULD LITERALLY DECAPITATE ME WITH A FINGERNAIL...

When your computer freezes, and the blue screen comes up saying to wait a while or press Ctl+Alt+Delete to restart the computer. So you hit Ctl+Alt+Delete, and after holding it down for a good ten seconds, you're left with the same feeling you'd have after a good ten days of government bureaucracy: "Why is nothing happening yet?"

So you end up shutting the thing down by the power button, and the next time you turn on the computer, it claims it "wasn't shut down properly." Fuck you! I did everything I was supposed to. You're the one who copped out, you Atari bastard offspring.

Why on *America's Funniest Home Videos* are the three finalist videos the stupidest ones they showed all night? It'll be a dog being sprayed by a hose, a redneck riding a bike into a mailbox, and some kid who's scared by a sock puppet and cries.

When I watch the Final Four on TV, why do they always have the ugliest colors possible painted on the court? Electric blues and greens and pinks. It looks like someone slaughtered a family of Muppets.

Where does low-grade, grocery-brand bottled water come from? Isn't water just water? I never thought it could actually taste bad. Then again, I never thought to drain my kid's inflatable pool and sell it, either.

When a local business runs the same annoying TV commercial for fifteen years just because they're too cheap to make a new one.

When you're speeding on a highway late at night and you think you see a cop on the side of the road so you jam on your brakes, your blood runs cold, and it turns out to just be an abandoned car.

When a bunch of presidential politicians take part in a state's primary elections and no matter what the results are, it sounds like everyone's a winner. The winner obviously claims victory, the runner-up more or less claims victory as well, third place is extremely confident with his strong showing, and fourth place sees the results as promising and vows to press on to other states where he or she will undoubtedly win. What is this, six-year-old T-ball? One person wins, and the rest should be sprayed down with a hose.

Why do some people say they can't take pills? Do you not have a throat?

Hotel or other bathrooms that have the light switch located outside the room. I've probably spent a combined six hours of my life feeling for bathroom switches that aren't even there.

When you want to listen to music while you run and every time a gust of wind blows, or you swing your arms, one of the fitted ear pieces falls out like a drifter from a freight train. Maybe next time you're designing headphones, you could do a little more than ramming your kid's Play-Doh in your ear, mailing it to a plastic factory, and calling it a day.

If one morning I woke up in hell, I wouldn't be able to tell the difference by the sound of that fucking thing.

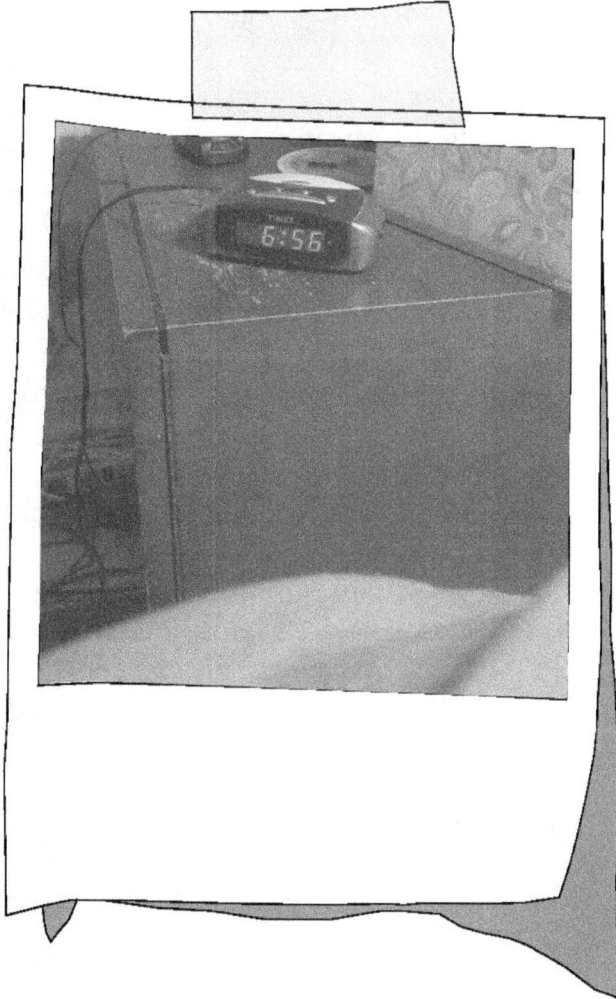

When you're driving down a road, trying to find some place you've never been to, and you realize you don't even know what street you're driving on at that moment. So every side street you pass, you look for the sign that identifies what street you're on and you end up passing ten or twelve streets and half a dozen prostitutes. None of them is much help either, because all they do is call you "honey" and tell you you're on "Easy Street."

Everywhere I go shopping, cashiers always ask me if I have a "such and such" card. "Do you have a Stop and Shop card?" "Do you have a CVS card?" "Do you have your V-card?" Believe me, if I had your fucking card I'd have whipped it out and waved it in your face from the moment I walked in the door. Then I would've found your store's card and shown that, too.

At the dentist when they cover your chest with a lead vest and then shoot an X-ray gun right at your head.

When you're showering in a hotel, and you turn around quickly, and your whole body sticks to the same shower curtain at least a dozen hairy men have also probably stuck to this month.

When someone is talking on a cell phone, the signal cuts out, and somehow he thinks something will change for the better between the seventh and eighth "hello?"

On *Wheel of Fortune* when people clap every time someone spins the wheel.

When you're surfing a news website and see a headline for a story you really want to read, and you click on the link, but it sends you to the wrong story or gives you one of those "warning: page has expired" screens. OK, it's expired, but why the warning? What exactly is the threat posed by a deceased website?

When you ask someone for relatively simple driving directions, and he goes on for ten minutes about every minute detail of the drive and repeats the whole thing three or four times.

"You want to go down the road and look for the orange mailbox. Then about a quarter mile after that on the left you'll see four medium-sized rocks. They're not very big, but they're not pebbles either, and one of them used to be painted red. Turn right at the first light, but not the second light. If you turn right at the second light, you'll see a dairy store with a big plastic cow out front, and you'll know you've gone the wrong way. Don't turn left at the second light, either, because that'll take you near old Willy's gas station and he puts down a lot of whiskey, and we don't think he's used up all the grenades he brought back from 'Nam. So don't turn there, and especially don't buy his milkshakes if you'll be driving very far
.   .   ."
"So I go down the street and take the   first   right."
"Yeah, but it's not as simple as you think . . ."

On Groundhog Day they pull the rodent out of its hole and say that if it sees its shadow there will be six more weeks of winter. So that implies if it doesn't see its shadow then spring will begin right away. When's the last time spring started on February 3rd in central Pennsylvania? Come to think of it, when's the last time spring started there six weeks later either? Why don't they move the whole thing to Philadelphia and replace it with a ceremony on April 1st where everyone gathers to watch the Philly Phanatic emerge from its lair of beer bottles in the bullpen, and realizes that baseball's going to start that week no matter what the stupid weather is?

Why does ghost traffic occur? You'll be on the highway and everyone slows down to thirty mph, so you guess there must be construction or an accident up ahead. Then, two minutes later, everyone is back up to sixty-five, and you're looking for emergency lights or orange cones—and nothing! Obviously, someone had to be the first to slow down. Why? Abrupt senility? Self-asphyxiating flatulence? Dropped another smoldering joint on your crotch? Guess we'll never know.

When a trendy song by a popular band comes on the radio and the person you're sitting next to starts ranting. He'll talk about how he loved that band and listened to their music a long time before anyone else did, and he used to go to concerts where he could stand right next to the stage, but now he can't even get tickets to a show. Then he'll turn to you like he wants some sort of sympathy. Then you'll think for a second, maybe about baseball.

Rappers or athletes who say they didn't choose to rap or play sports but that rap or sports chose them.

I hate movie scenes about airplanes fighting in midair. It's not like a sports scene or fighting on the ground where you have a sense of who's who. Once they're up in the planes, it's just like, what the fuck is going on? You can't really root for someone because you don't have a clue where anyone is. Then all of a sudden, the scene's over, and someone's the winner, and he's strutting around with a cigar. OK, hot shot, you want your Johnson tugged now or at the end of the movie?

Songs on the radio with background noises that sound like cell phones. I'll be driving down the highway, and some rap song will come on with a bunch of beeping in the background. I'll turn off the radio and listen. Then I'll think that maybe I just missed a call, so I'll look through the seat cracks for my phone. Then I'll find it and look at the phone's screen. Then I'll strap my helmet on a little tighter.

Every week, I have to listen to a special report about scientists who *may* have discovered a new kind of food that *may* help *reduce* the risk of *some* cancers. Things like a glass of wine, chocolate, pizza, fruit juice, sawdust, and a toddler's feces. Look, if you're willing to rationalize to yourself that eating Hershey bars and drinking until you can't walk every night will somehow absolve you from the threat of cancer, there are probably more serious issues you need to address before worrying about phantom, yet-to-be tumors.

Fat people who order two double cheeseburgers, a plate of French fries, a chocolate brownie sundae, and a Diet Coke. If I hear you so much as hint that you're not losing weight from that Diet Coke, I will smack you over the head with one of your chins.

When you're listening to a call-in radio show, and you hear guys call in with all kinds of praise and thanks for the host and wishing him and his family the best. These sick people call in every week and try to act like they're best friends with the host, and they'll even apologize if they haven't called in a few days because they were out of town fishing with their sons ages nine and twelve and he just wants to ask a follow up question to one he first called in three years ago . . .

Does the issue of where humans came from and how it's taught in schools keep you up at night? You honestly wonder how some of these people make it through the day. Is it offensive to hear I descended from some monkey while plenty of those assholes are still hanging around? Sure, but it's not a given to believe the couple who appeared from thin air faster than O.J.'s "real killers." Yet somehow I accept this as one of many questions I will never be able to answer, and find a way to move on.

When you're trying to watch something on TV that you really want to hear, but someone else nearby won't stop talking to you. You don't want to hush the person, so you just sort of lean closer to the TV, squint your eyes, and let five or ten seconds elapse before you respond to each question. Some people just can't take a hint though, and that's when it's time to fight volume with volume. Get comfortable on that couch, too, because it's probably where you'll be sleeping for a while.

If every time you go to the doctor's office they make you wait twenty minutes, why don't they just tell you to come twenty minutes later?

When a burn from hot pizza numbs your mouth.

B
oring

C
ranky

S
tubborn

WHY DO THINGS HAVE TO CHANGE?
I GIVE A SHIT WHO WINS THE "LYSOL
TOILET BOWL!" DAMN YOU KIDS AND YOUR
CHANGE... I HAVEN'T CHANGED MY
UNDERWEAR IN THREE WEEKS AND
NO ONE'S COMPLAINED
YET..!

I'm tired of these recliner sports experts who preach that it's impossible to have a college football playoff system. It's more than obvious that, given the choice, any sports fan would choose a playoff system over what's already been tried. So in order to separate themselves from the naïve masses and give themselves an intellectual boost, these guys side with the current system, and list all of the reasons a college football playoff wouldn't work. The problem is, any reason they list is easily undermined with a little thing called rational thought. Take a look at the existing championship schedule on the next page.

Now the first thing you'll notice is that there's no plausible reason why a playoff couldn't be held in between when the current regular season ends and when the current championship game is played. So the armchair experts will begin pulling other reasons from their asses to explain why a playoff can't be held during a five-week span.

"If you start adding more games, the schedule will become too long, and it's unreasonable to ask something so demanding of college athletes."

Comparatively speaking, college football teams play the same number, or fewer, games than high school teams play in a full season, including playoffs. High school teams could play an eleven to seventeen-game schedule, whereas a college team currently never exceeds fourteen. Adding one to three games to a college team's thirteen game season would raise the number of games a team could play to sixteen, and that's only for the two teams reaching the finals.

Not to mention, no one's being forced to play extra playoff games; if you told 12-0 Utah or Boise State that if they played in two or three more games they could legitimately claim a national title, as opposed to being just another asterisk in the history books, do you

M	T	W	TH	F	S	S	
NOVEMBER							
1	2	3	4	5	6	7	
8	9	10	11	12	13	14	
15	16	17	18	19	20	21	
22	23	24	25	26	27	28	
29	30						
DECEMBER							
		1	2	3	4	5	
6	7	8	9	10	11	12	1
13	14	15	16	17	18	19	2
20	21	22	23	24	25	26	3
27	28	29	30	31			
JANUARY							
					1	2	4
3	4	5	6	7	8	9	5
10	11						

Current regular season	
Current conference championship games	
Idle weeks for teams playing in final	
Current bowl game period	
Current BCS bowl game period	
Current national championship game	

honestly see anyone in those programs saying, "I really think you're asking too much of us now, we've played the season we were required to, and now we'd just like to go home"?

Next reason: "It's completely unreasonable to expect major college football programs, after a grueling regular season, to pick up and play up to three playoff games in neutral stadiums across the country. Between the logistics of money, fatigue, and transporting fan bases that far, that quickly, it could never happen."

Who said playoff games need to be at neutral sites? Just because college basketball does a playoff a certain way doesn't mean it's right for any other sport.

"With a playoff format, if the number one team played the number two team in the last week of the regular season, neither team would have the motivation to play their first string; they would simply put in their second string and rest the starters for the postseason."

If there was a four-team playoff only the top seed would be guaranteed home field advantage until the neutral-site final. In a sport where this advantage arguably has the greatest impact on the game itself, especially at the college level, the number one and number two seeds would be fighting tooth and nail to secure that top seed.

Even in an eight or twelve-team format, again, only the top four teams would be guaranteed a home game; if any of the prospective top seeds lost a regular season game by enough points, that team could easily fall far enough in the rankings to lose home field advantage and be forced to play the postseason on the road.

"If you hold a playoff in December the student-athletes won't be able to study for and focus on their December finals, which is the real reason they're in school to begin with."

Aside from the fact that you don't even believe what you just said, why would football have such a difficult time managing this hurdle when other sports deal with finals without major issues every semester? Basketball, lacrosse, and baseball all have seasons during final exams, and each of those sports has more games and more travel to deal with than football.

Take a look at the calendar on the opposite page. This is a simple example of a college football playoff. The week after the conference championship games, the four seed would play at the one seed, and the three seed at the two seed. Not complicated at all.

"College football will never give up the bowl system because of monetary interests; enough programs get enough economic benefits from the current format that no one involved will want to change it, especially to a playoff format where the money would be divided up more between every Division I-A program."

Who said the present bowl system needs to change? I say leave it exactly the way it is: the same bowls, on the same dates, in the same places, with the same sponsors, the same TV rights, and the same payouts. That way, no one can complain about losing money by shifting to a different system. The only difference is that instead of a computer picking which teams play in the championship game, the teams themselves would settle the matter on the field by mid-December. The teams that lost during the playoff could enter the running for other bowl games like they otherwise would, and would still have a chance to end the season on a high note; that way, coaches could enjoy the opportunity of ending the season with a bowl win and a trophy to impress potential recruits with, as they always have.

There's also one final point that's difficult to manage when it comes to arguing against a playoff:

NOVEMBER							
M	**T**	**W**	**TH**	**F**	**S**	**S**	
1	2	3	4	5	6	7	
8	9	10	11	12	13	14	
15	16	17	18	19	20	21	
22	23	24	25	26	27	28	
29	30						
DECEMBER							
		1	2	3	4	5	
6	7	8	9	10	11	12	
13	14	15	16	17	18	19	1
20	21	22	23	24	25	26	2
27	28	29	30	31			3
JANUARY							
					1	2	
3	4	5	6	7	8	9	4
10	11						

Current regular season	▨
Current conference championship games	≡
4 seed at 1 seed / 3 seed at 2 seed	▧
Idle weeks for teams playing in final	▥
Current bowl game period	▨
Current BCS bowl game period	≡
Current national championship game	▨

Football playoffs are already in place in every other college sports division and they operate without any issues, and everyone enjoys them very much.

So in the broadest of terms, if the bowls stood as they are, and the playoff were added to supplement the bowl system, not only would money not be lost by those who benefit from the current system, but there would be a tremendous amount of extra income infused into the system. Simply having a four-team playoff creates an extra home game for two teams, and the television rights to those games would easily be equal in value to any present BCS bowl game. How the cash is divided from these extra games is up to the NCAA to decide for itself, but when there's more money to be made, no matter how small your share of the additional income is, it's hard to reason turning that down. Not to mention, this is only based on the simplest of playoff formats. Think about the income potential of a larger playing field, like the one shown on the opposite page.

Imagine a format similar to this, in which the week following the conference championship games became a college football juggernaut: Quarter-final games at noon, three, six, and nine. Fans could also enjoy two semi-final games the following weekend, and three full weeks of bowl games leading up to the national title match in January. Yes the playoffs might overlap with the beginning of bowl season, but the losers of the playoff games aren't going to move on to the Metamucil.com Bowl, they'll be playing in the higher profile bowls, which don't begin until after the new year.

So, whatever a playoff system eventually looks like, once the current postseason contract is up, what's there to lose? Besides the chance to make more money, eliminate computer controversy, and make every paying customer of the industry much, much happier?

NOVEMBER							
M	*T*	*W*	*TH*	*F*	*S*	*S*	
1	2	3	4	5	6	7	
8	9	10	11	12	13	14	
15	16	17	18	19	20	21	
22	23	24	25	26	27	28	
29	30						
DECEMBER							
		1	2	3	4	5	
6	7	8	9	10	11	12	
13	14	15	16	17	18	19	
20	21	22	23	24	25	26	1
27	28	29	30	31			
JANUARY							
					1	2	2
3	4	5	6	7	8	9	3
10	11						

Current regular season	
Current conference championship games	
8 seed at 1 seed / 7 seed at 2 seed **6 seed at 3 seed / 5 seed at 4 seed**	
Lower seed winners at higher seed winners	
Idle weeks for teams playing in final	
Current bowl game period	
Current BCS bowl game period	
Current national championship game	

Congratulations pigeon, you're the only stupid bird that actually looks out of place in nature and not in a urine-speckled, gum-crusted gutter. Dinosaurs would be proud to see what their genes have produced.

When there's some kind of tragedy like a natural disaster, and it's all over the news day in and day out. Then, a week later, some news channel will play a minute-long commercial bragging about how they were the first to bring you the most in-depth information and reporting about the event, and how they crushed the competition. Do you think you could spare hoisting a trophy in the face of a tragedy that has clearly ruined hundreds or thousands of people's lives?

Why does there have to be a graduation for every grade in school now? I don't mind an excuse to get drunk at a BBQ, but the pageantry begins to wear a little thin when you've already graduated three times before high school.

When you're at a gym spotting someone doing bench presses who has awful breath, and every time he pumps a rep, you get a blast of dead raccoon in your face.

If you sleep through a complimentary breakfast at a hotel, shouldn't you get the money back for it?

There are entirely too many numbers being retired in professional sports. Did anyone stop to think that if some teams keep it up, sooner or later players are going to be wearing zip codes on their uniforms? Number shortages aside, the whole criteria behind retiring numbers rub me the wrong way. I like teams that have retired only one or two numbers in their existence, but some have close to a dozen numbers forever crossed-off the team roster. Just because a player is popular now doesn't mean any fan down the line will be able to put a face, or even an achievement, along with the name. Imagine players a hundred years from now trying to pick out their numbers and being told the one they want is retired. Will anyone be able to explain offhand the reason why?

When you find a song on the radio that you love but it isn't coming in too well and gets mixed up with another station. Then your passenger goes ahead and changes the station when you were perfectly content listening to static for three minutes just because you love the song so much.

On TV when they show a close-up of someone holding the Super Bowl trophy and it's covered with smudge marks from people's fingers.

When you buy warm beer sitting out in a store display, but you want to drink the beers right away. So you think to put them in the freezer at home for ten minutes to make them cold really fast. Then you wander over to the TV and start watching reruns of the 1982 World Series. Then you look at the clock two hours later. Then you remember them brews.

When you're waiting for an episode of a TV show to come on, and they try to squeeze a commercial in between the introduction and the start of the show.

People who continuously snort mucus back into their noses rather than using a tissue to blow it out.

Disturbingly-perky toll booth attendants.

Obese people who wear anything less than a mascot suit to the beach.

I hate it when two people have a conversation over the phone. Not a normal call where two people hold phones to their heads and converse. I mean when one of the phone-holders acts as a relay person to a third individual standing to the side. One or two comments are fine, but when it goes on for a minute and a half, just hand the damn phone over! None of this, "…Well, Patty says . . . well, Dick says . . . Patty says . . . Dick says . . . Patty says . . . Dick says . . ." Screw Dick and screw Patty. Or let Dick screw Patty. I hear Patty likes Dick.

When you're in a hurry trying to print out one thing from a website that seems like it would only take ten seconds to print, but it takes forever because it prints out all five pages of the website, including that last page that has only one line of crap at the top.

Have you ever been driving in the rain with your wipers on, and twenty minutes later your wipers are still on but it stopped raining a long time ago, and you realize you're the only winner who still has them on?

People who are afraid of riding on roller-coasters. I mean, if you're afraid of getting sick or have a medical condition, that's one thing, but if you're just plain scared, what's the big deal? You stand there for twenty minutes watching perfectly happy people get on and off the thing, a lot of them probably aren't even old enough to drive, and you just stand there like a wooden Indian at a cigar store. Why did you even come to an amusement park?

People who tell me their computers have a certain number of megabits, gigs, migs, or trilobites, and then wait for me to sound impressed. Computers are like cars. I really don't care as long as they work.

Tennis players who grunt every time they hit a ball.

When you're in a hurry to shut down your computer and you fail to notice that it's set for "restart" and not "shut down" when you click OK.

When you're at an awards show and the MC says to please hold your applause until after an entire group of recipients has been announced, and after the first name on the list is read, everyone bursts into applause anyway.

When you want someone to take a picture of you with your digital camera and she says no, it's ok, she'll just use her camera and email you the picture. This sounds nice and all, but no one EVER emails the pictures. People probably aren't doing it on purpose, but they get caught up with their lives and forget. So, not to sound rude and all, but I INSIST you use my camera. Don't look through all the pictures on there though. Did I mention you look fat in the shower?

When a group of people is watching a moving scene from a famous movie, and everyone wants to just sit there and take it in, except for that guy. That guy who feels so insecure about watching something serious on TV with other people that he launches into a comedic play-by-play of the scene. While everyone wants to just watch, he won't shut up with the wisecracks and one-liners every ten seconds. Then he'll add that cackling weasel laugh and look around for approval. The thing to keep in mind is that this guy will receive a beating within an inch of his life someday. It is inevitable, and I cherish that fact.

Don't you hate it when the coach of the NFL team you're rooting for decides to challenge a play early in a half, on like second down, that doesn't have any particular significance, and loses the stupid challenge?

What exactly is a voluntary evacuation? Some tropical storm comes barreling up the coast, and authorities announce there's a voluntary evacuation. Either you're having an evacuation or you're not. If you want people to get the hell out, just say so! Aren't we always in a state of voluntary evacuation? People can leave whenever they want. Just wait outside a Baltimore Orioles game around the fourth inning, and you'll see what I'm talking about.

When sports fans talk about their favorite team using the pronoun "we."
"We almost lost last night, but then we pulled together and came through in double overtime." If you didn't suit up for the game, I don't want to hear about it.

During basketball games when a player is taking two consecutive foul shots, and in between each shot, every player on the shooter's team has to make some kind of physical contact with the shooter's body: a handshake, a high five, or a slap on the ass. All the while, the entire crowd and TV audience roll their eyes and wonder how long this groping session will last before everyone in the arena who wants to has congratulated the shooter on his first attempt and wished him best of luck on his upcoming attempt.

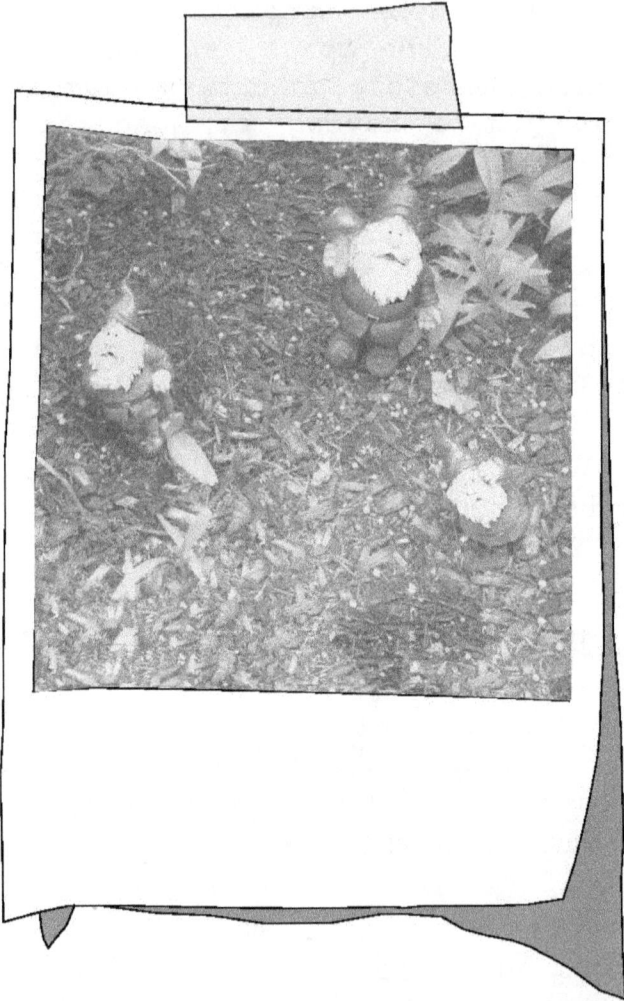

Woo woo!
Next stop on the
train to dementia:
Littering your property
with life-size replicas
of Santa's extramarital
bastard children...

When someone with grey hair is required by some asinine, heavy-handed, meddlesome rule to provide identification when buying alcohol.

Protestors who have to be dragged away. Protesting is a great way to make a point, but when it comes to forming human chains or refusing to move when the cops come, your image starts to lose some credibility. I mean, how can you take someone seriously who has to be carried away, kicking and crying, by four officers? There's a time to make a point, and there's a time to call it a day, and that time is when two hundred men with nightsticks show up.

When you think you turned off your alarm in the morning, and you get out of bed and hop in the shower. Then thirty seconds later, you realize you only hit the snooze button, and you either have to run soaking wet to turn it off or take the whole damn shower with the buzzer going in the background.

Why did painters hundreds of years ago feel the need to paint fat, naked women? Don't tell me these women were attractive in their time, because they weren't, they're fat. These gals have pot bellies that put professional bowlers to shame.

When you're watching a baseball game on TV, and some guy comes up to bat and fouls off eleven or twelve pitches, takes about twenty minutes doing it, and really drives up the suspense of what's going to finally happen. Then he grounds into a double play to end the inning and doesn't even run it out.

When it comes to poker, why does every sap tell you the same thing? "I'm a good player, but sometimes I just make some really stupid mistakes." Good players don't make really stupid mistakes.

When you're flipping through TV channels, and one station's volume is a lot lower than the stations around it. So you turn the volume up to watch one show for a while, then you change the channel, and NOW YOU CAN SEE THAT NOT ONLY DOES IT STAY SHARP, BUT THE MIRACLE BLADE HAS JUST CUT STRAIGHT THROUGH THE COUNTER. IT CAN ALSO CUT MY ASSISTANT INTO THIRTY SLICES, AND HE WILL STAY IN THAT FORM UNTIL HE BENDS TO SIT ON THE JOHN . . .

When people who speak English as their first language go to a foreign country where other people clearly don't know English, yet proceed to ask long, complicated questions in English anyway. You'll be at a restaurant where the waitress struggled to understand "bottled water," and you'll hear someone say, "Yes, I'd like the beef and stirred rice, please. But could I get brown rice instead of white rice, and could I have the beef cooked medium-well, not medium. I'd also like a side plate of green beans, not on the same plate as the main course, and could I have a bit of butter with the beans as well. Thank you." Then, five minutes later: "Well, this isn't what I ordered! Excuse me, miss?"

When there are plenty of open seats at a theatre, or a ballgame, and some guy shows up late with the usher and insist that the two people sitting in his seats get up and move to two of the three hundred nearby empty seats.

When the knob on a hotel shower is so sensitive that it takes ten minutes of going back and forth trying to get the right temperature before you finally just give up and go back to bed.

When you're relieving yourself in a public bathroom, and you look down to see a motivational message printed on the urinal mat like, "Don't do drugs." Who would've guessed that the most inspirational place to convince me to salvage my life would be at the bottom of a urinal?

People who cut up plastic six-pack can holders before throwing them out so a fish won't get stuck in them.

When you go to a foreign country and it's explained by your tour guide and tour books that tipping isn't customary, but people still give you a nasty look like they were expecting one anyway.

The smell left on your hands by a wet sponge.

Have you ever seen pop-up ads on your computer that offer you two buttons to click? One will be big and colorful, and says, "Tell me more!" The other will be small and gray, and says, "No, thanks." Do you ever get annoyed at the polite words they try to put in your mouth? How 'bout a button that says, "Eat shit, you infected horse hemorrhoid"?

Have you ever been looking at someone's face as they talk and felt like you should be at a carnival trying to hit it with a mallet?

Faking interest in a barber's dull, endless story.

How about after you check out at a store and walk fifteen feet to the exit, and you have to show your receipt to some underpaid, apathetic clerk who clearly saw you just buy everything that's in your cart. Then he looks down at the receipt like he's checking the winning Play 4 combo, and indifferently mumbles that you're good to go. Thanks.

The program for text messages on cell phones that tries to anticipate what you want to say and fills in a sentence for you. For example, you try to write, "I'll be over as soon as nine," and end up with "I'll bet you eat steak like you eat an asshole."

When you meet someone for the first time and you're not sure whether or not to shake the person's hand. If it's a business or family introduction, it's pretty clear that a handshake is the proper thing to do. But how about when your friend introduces you to someone at a bar who you're probably not going to talk to that night, and you'll never see again? Then if there is a handshake, it becomes an issue of who instigates it: If they're different sexes, is it the man or the woman? The older person or the younger? The taller or the shorter? And what if the guy only has a left arm and you're right-handed? Do you pretend to be left-handed, or do you just go for a high five and hope for the best?

College or government buildings that have letters engraved in stone. That's because instead of chiseling the letter "u" they'll put a "v." It'll say something like "Those stvdents who enter vpon this campvs have svre earned the privilege." Just because the Romans did it doesn't make you sophisticated.

Tom Petty once sang, "You can stand me up to the gates of hell, but I won't back down." Bullshit. Have you ever opened an oven that's 400 degrees? Hot as fuck. Now image the gates of hell. Back down in a fucking second.

SINCE WE'RE BOTH INTERESTED IN DOING THE WORLD A FAVOR RIGHT NOW, COULD YOU GO AHEAD AND RECYCLE MY ICED-TEA BOTTLE WHEN YOU GET A CHANCE? THANKS.

LESS MISERABLE COMMUTERS

GETTING IN TOUCH WITH MOTHER EARTH

When a loading pop-up ad crashes your Internet Explorer.

What's the hype about flavored water? It's the most disgusting thing I've ever tasted. Water is a necessity, not a liquid delicacy.

Why do I always have to ask for a knife at a Chinese restaurant? Clearly, they already have knives somewhere, so what's the big holdup with putting them out to begin with? No one's starting a revolution out here, I'm just having a little trouble with General Tso.

When anti-virus software brings your computer to a screeching halt as it tries to scan its own upgrade that it forced you to download in the first place.

When you're watching TV with the volume on really low because someone else is sleeping nearby, and every time a commercial comes on, you have to find the remote and press "mute" because for some reason it's still legal in this country for the volume of television commercials to induce internal bleeding in the ear canals of viewers.

When you go to another country for vacation and all a local wants to do is jabber your ear off about politics. But it's really not a discussion, it's that person lecturing you on why he's right and America's wrong.

Listen, if I wanted to talk politics, I could have stayed at home and found a chat room to argue in all day. Believe it or not, I'm actually visiting your country to relax, take in some sights, and, well, enjoy myself. So why don't you take the dog-and-pony show to another pub or, better yet, check up on what your own country is doing once in a while instead of spending all day finding flaws with mine.

Case-sensitive computer passwords. First I have to memorize ten different passwords: one for each email address, one for work, one for eBay, one for Amazon, and one for PayPal. Obviously, I want to use the same password for everything, but I know if I do that, some hacker will get it, access everything, and shove a steel credit dildo up my ass.

So I bother to write down all the different passwords and have them on yellow Post-it notes all over the house. Then when I finally start to remember them, I can't recall which letters are capitals and which aren't, and I'm back to square one.

Why can't we have retinal scans? Or voice activation? Or even a dog wired to the hard drive that sniffs your crotch for ID. Anything but this compulsive, neurotic infatuation with asking for a password with TWO UPPERCASE LETTERS, two lowercase letters, at least 1 number, and a symbol!, but without using any proper nouns, adjectives, profanities, or other words susceptible to simple rote memorization. Passwords like b!tE m3.

When you're mailing a parking ticket and you seal the ticket inside the envelope before writing down the address to send it to.

When you're mailing something at the post office and the person behind the counter asks if you need to pay for the envelope that you clearly just took off the shelf next to the counter.

If so many people want to lose weight, but they all say they don't have enough time to exercise, then why don't they just eat *less* of what they're eating? Time does not hinder anyone from consuming less than they normally do. So if you eat three brownie sundaes every day and you cut back to two, while engaging in the same level of physical activity, then you're going to lose weight.

In *The Empire Strikes Back*, right after Darth Vader tells Luke he's his father, Luke jumps off the ledge, falls about a thousand feet, and comes away without a scratch. Well, what the fuck is that?

People who knee-jerk correct you for any slight exaggeration or wrong fact you use in a discussion whether it's relevant to the point or not.

When you're woken up early in the morning on vacation by the sound of construction work.

The next time soda companies try to raise the price of soda at vending machines I'm going to raise hell. Honestly, at 75 cents or a dollar a pop, you'd think a twelve-pack would be about $10. No, it costs $4.89! That works out to 40 cents a soda, not including the cost of the box, and they're still making a profit. Sometimes I don't have much to do, but my computer came with a calculator.

When you have a wallet or cell phone in your pocket while sitting on an airplane, and it constantly jams against the reclining button. You get sent flying backward more than an AA meeting at the Heineken brewery.

When you get in an argument with someone who pulls out poll numbers and percentages to use as facts against you. Poll numbers are a sample taken from the general public, and since when was anything the general public thought about worth considering for an argument?

The people who say not to judge a book by its cover are the same yodels who come back later and say you should've trusted your gut instinct.

When you're standing in line for a sandwich at a deli and some rectal deposit won't get off his phone when it's his turn to order. The poor guy behind the counter keeps asking what kind of bread and cheese the guy wants. With each question, the sandwich-maker has to yank this sack of phlegm away from his phone, and the guy always sounds annoyed.

"What? Um, I don't know, white bread . . . What? Look, whatever, give me some cheese . . . What? I don't know . . . Sorry, what were you saying, Hank?"

Just because the guy's making the sandwich in front of you doesn't mean there isn't a stack of bread he's already wiped his ass with waiting under the counter for customers like yourself.

When you say you got a haircut and someone replies, "Just one?"

Fancy restaurants that charge a lot of money for very little food. Have you ever eaten at one of these places? A steak costs $40, and it turns out to be two pieces of meat on a stick with some parsley. It's a brilliant scam, and I applaud the entrepreneurs who capitalize on customers' empty quests for self-empowerment in an endless attempt to consider themselves *trendy*.

What's with all these lines on the road that look like someone drove over them five seconds after they were painted? Doesn't anybody block off the road for an hour so the paint can dry?

Have you ever had to sit through some nativity play put on by a bunch of first or second graders, and wondered when they bring out the Cabbage Patch doll and put it in the manger if a really awkward sex talk took place at rehearsal between all of the kids and the poor schmuck who was asked where real babies come from? It's amusing enough to wonder what answer the responsible adult provided to at least occupy your mind through the rest of the play. I bet it was either a fire-and-brimstone response or a smartass one, i.e., sex is evil and so are you, or you came by UPS, now keep quiet or I'll ship you back.

When airlines don't stock up enough of the one choice of meal everyone's obviously going to pick. They always run out of lasagna, and I either have to go hungry or eat the fish. It's like somewhere they have a monkey with an inner ear disorder making these decisions.

Men who wear fur coats. Exactly what point are you trying to make? I already know you're an asshole, so what else could it be?

When you're trying to watch a baseball game, and they slap a headset on the manager while he's trying to coach and start yapping away with questions. The whole time you can see the guy's just trying to watch what's going on and you feel sorry for him, and just want to tell the announcers to shut up and leave this man alone.

When you open up a magazine and have to flip through ten or twelve pages of advertisements just to reach the table of contents.

People who complain about gas prices, and then walk into the Mini Mart, buy a large slushy, a Snickers bar, a pack of cigarettes, two lottery tickets, and wonder why they still have holes in their socks.

When you try to tell some dolt he has a crumb on his cheek and you point to one of your cheeks and he points to his cheek, too.

When people kiss their slimy babies right after they're born.

When you're trying to read a book and the author starts introducing a bunch of characters with similar names. The way I remember characters in a book is by their initials, so I read "Franky Toughnuts" and remember "FT." Sometimes I'll even just go by the first letter of the first name. I'll read "Mickey Smallpeck" and remember "M." So I'll read sixty or seventy pages and realize I'm confused out of my mind. Then I'll start looking closely at the names and find out who I thought was one person is actually three or four different characters with the same initials. That's when I close the book and open a beer.

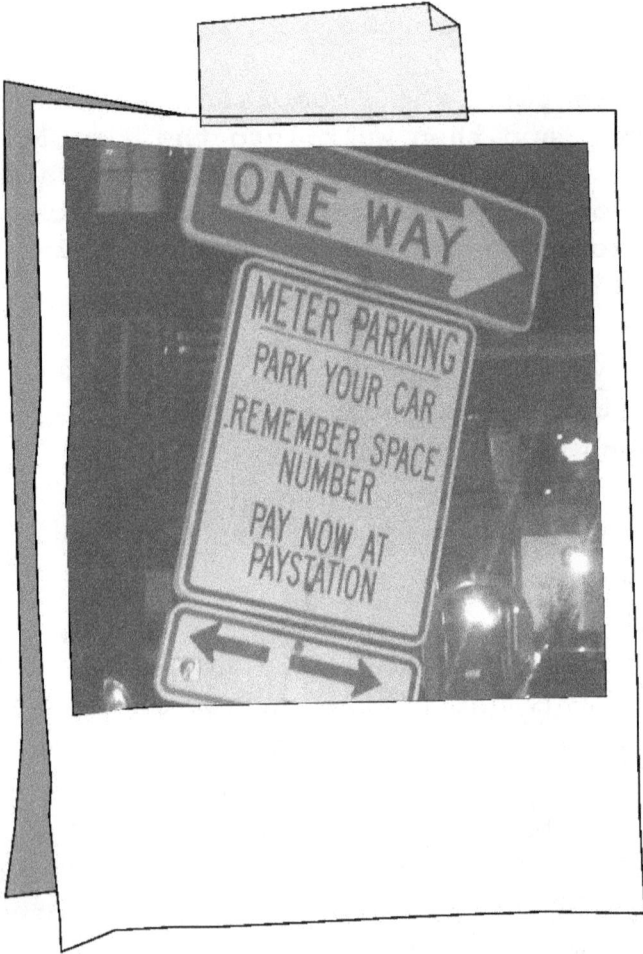

Sure! We're happy to help phase-out parking meters by bringing cash to one faraway spot instead of inconveniencing you to walk around and fetch it.
Would you like me to stop for your drycleaning too? Need anything at the hardware store? I could even stand in your room with a bedpan the next time you have the runs! Just let me know!

Stories on the news about the first baby born in the new year. So what? How long 'til he can mow my lawn?

Have you ever received a survey in the mail from some hotel you stayed at a month ago? The damn thing is six pages long! Please rate on a scale of 1 to 10 the quality of your pillow's firmness. Please rate on a scale of 1 to 10 the soothing effect the carpet had on your mood during the first twenty minutes in your room. Please rate on a scale of 1 to 10 the likelihood that the man behind the desk was fondling himself prior to dispensing your room key. If answer was 5 or higher, please indicate in less than three paragraphs whether you suspect same-race, inter-racial, or inter-species porn was playing in the staff room.

Don't you love it when the media start reporting on reporters? Like when one of the networks gets a new anchorperson, you'll hear all the reporters discuss how they think the new anchor is going to do. Then the anchor will be on the front page of all the papers, and the day after his or her first show, all the news websites and magazines will be discussing and critiquing every aspect of the "performance."

I guess my question is: why are people who present the news in the news itself just for doing their jobs? If a network news anchor carjacked a retired couple and went on a six-day cocaine-and-paint-thinner binge and woke up covered in Pop Tart and condom wrappers in a motel room next to a one-armed male escort, then the anchor's actions would be newsworthy for a night. As for critiquing anchorpersons' jobs, like it's Oscar season in Tinsel Town, can you spare me the hype and just get to the news?

When you flip to some movie on TV that you've never seen before and someone else walks in the room two minutes later and starts barking questions to you about the plot. No matter how many times you tell the person you don't know, because you've only been watching for two minutes, the questions never stop.

When a few people are sitting together, and each one is talking about a completely different subject. Everyone's speaking, but no one's listening! It'll go like this:
Ray: "But Susan didn't really love the man I caught her sleeping with, because she slept with me right after him." *Pause*
Cathy: "Yeah, I might be able to buy some cheap curtains if that place by Macy's is still open." *Pause*
Tim: "I mean I just can't understand it. How could I win so many sweepstakes in a single day?" *Pause*
Ray: "But then she slept with the cable guy after me. Come to think of it, that woman sleeps with anything that moves."

Golfers who don't fix divots when they probably hit the divots further than their balls to begin with.

TV ads that tell you everything you could possibly want to know about a drug and then tell you to go see their ads in a magazine. You just told me the answer to every question I could possibly have about your product, so why would I actively seek out to subject myself to another advertisement?

Why is so much hype built-up around the Heisman Trophy every year? No one cares about MVPs of professional sports for more than a few minutes, so why do I have to endure, year in and year out, listening to grown men drone on for hours, giving verbal blow jobs to the most deserving Heisman hopefuls for months on end? Because it's conversation? So were the internet chat logs Chris Hansen used to read on *To Catch a Predator*, but that didn't make those a healthy activity.

People who casually use the word "Genesis."

There's a difference between a fair and equal system and equal and balanced results; and there's no such thing as a completely fair system anyway.

When you're watching highlights of a game on *Sportscenter* and the final score for that game flashes across the ticker on the bottom of the screen before the highlights are finished.

People who overuse the word "my."

WHY I STOPPED WATCHING MOVIES ON REGULAR ← T.V.

Men's and women's brains are simply wired differently when it comes to meal-time conversation. Women seem to have no difficulty discussing topics during meals that would make the average man's food appear less appetizing than field day at a camp for fat kids.

Perhaps this is based on the theory that men's brains are more visually based, whereas women's are more language-based. Personally, I don't have an answer, but I do know that chafed legs, urination frequency, stool discolorations, and the always reliable grading of the restaurant's bathroom, and comparisons of that facility to other infamous bathrooms of the past, are all topics I've heard before that didn't appear to phase the appetites of women at the table, whereas on each occasion I felt more nauseous than I would have at a geriatric adult film festival.

Why are there so many "Judge" shows on TV? Are there really that many people willing to go to court on daytime television? I mean the only people who would think to volunteer in the first place are the same people who watch the show, and you'd think that they'd catch on from watching beforehand that people on the show always come across looking like morons. Maybe I shouldn't be thinking too deeply about the subject. I know they aren't.

Don't you feel a little violated when you go shopping, or to the movies, and you come outside to find a flyer on your windshield? Why not just dump the paper in the parking lot from the start and at least save me from doing half the work?

When you do a five-hundred-piece puzzle and don't realize until the end that two of the pieces are missing.

Bartenders at extremely crowded bars who pay no attention to which areas of the bar have recently been served. Most of the bartenders I encounter do a great job, and I tip them accordingly, but every now and then one of them just leaves me scratching my head.

One time, after twenty minutes of quietly waiting at the front of a bar and holding out a $20 bill as far as I could, I complained out loud about the service to the people around me and the chump standing next to me says, "Hey, I'm a bartender, they're trying really hard."

Yes, they are working very hard, but they're paying no attention to how long certain areas around the bar have been waiting patiently for their service.

If you're bartending at a packed bar, don't just stand continuously in one spot and serve whoever walks into your five-foot radius. At least fake that you're paying attention to whether the person you're attending to has been waiting for almost an entire half of a football game, or whether you're about to serve some prick everyone else just watched stroll right up to the bar.

Why do they bother to put public announcement systems in places where it's too loud to understand them anyway?

Why do punt and kickoff returners in football always stop running hard and try to finesse their way back and forth between the sidelines? Save it for your cash-strapped appearance on *Dancing With the Stars* in ten years, and run straight down the damn field.

Microwave meals never tell you to heat up the food for long enough. Half the time when you bite into the thing, it's still frozen inside. I already knew the food came out of your ass; apparently the cooking time does, too.

Why do women always go to the bathroom with a partner? Are you squeezing in some bench press on your way back?

Red light traffic cameras.

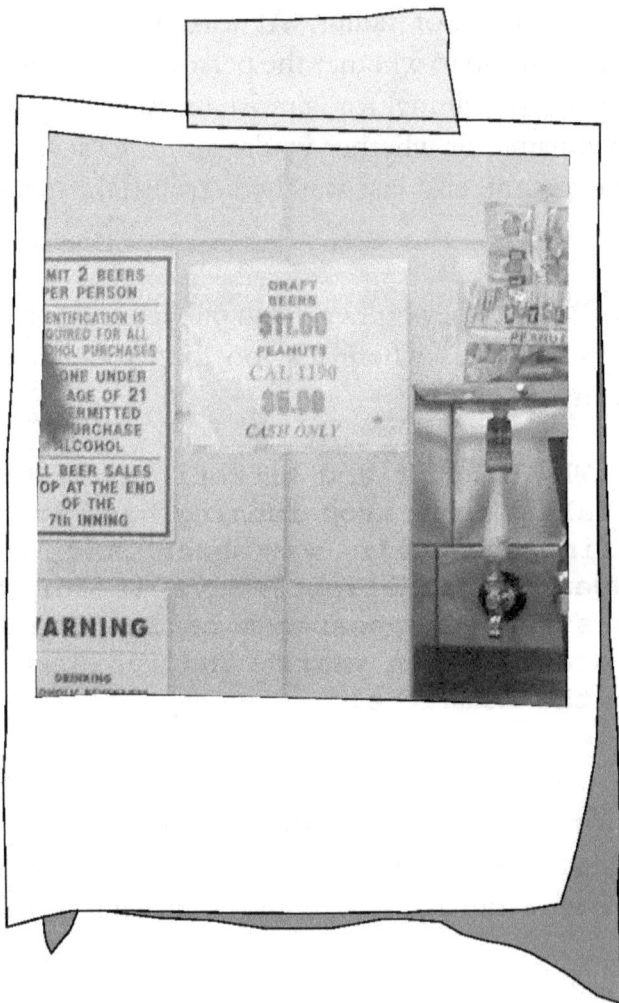

When a flock of geese flies over your car, and one of them relieves an urge on your windshield. It's comforting to know how often their flock must be hit by waste from airplane toilets.

Can someone explain what is gained by seatbelt buckles in the backseats of cars that only work when each tab is matched with the correct slot? The slots are labeled "left," "center," and "right," and each will accept only the corresponding tab. I think seatbelts should be promiscuous by nature: any old buckle should do.

People who complain that the United States has no culture. America is barely two hundred and thirty years old. Show me another country that came as far as we have in its first two centuries. They most certainly did not have *COPS* marathons by then.

When you lie down on grass without a shirt on and the skin on your back starts itching like you're a crackhead.

When you type a word like "fajitas" in a word processing program and it underlines the word in red, but you can't figure out why. So you right-click on the word to see if it's spelled incorrectly, and the suggestion it gives you is "fajita." I do believe that makes less sense than Happy Hour at a halfway house.

When a cell phone is set to vibrate, and it rings on a wood table nearby and scares the shit out of you.

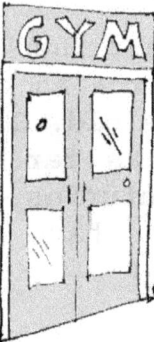

...AND THE WHOLE THING MIGHT BE INSPIRATIONAL IF ANY OF US HAD A LEGITIMATE, LASTING MOTIVATION TO BE HERE, OTHER THAN A NUMBER ON A CALENDAR THAT PASSED WEEKS AGO, WHICH HAS NO SIGNIFICANCE OF ITS OWN... UNLIKE, FOR EXAMPLE, ANY MORNING IN THE PAST 364 DAYS WHEN I SAW MYSELF NAKED IN THE MIRROR AND COULD HAVE SAID: "HUH, I AM REALLY UNHAPPY WITH HOW I LOOK..." AND THEN USED THAT AS MOTIVATION TO GET IN SHAPE...

COLA

..BUT INSTEAD OF PRODUCING ANY TANGIBLE RESULTS, I'VE COME IN THREE OR FOUR TIMES SINCE NEW YEAR'S DAY TO LOUNGE ON MACHINES, FLEX IN THE MIRROR, SUCK IN MY STOMACH, AND OTHERWISE SHOW THE DETERMINATION OF DISEASED LIVESTOCK

CHIK'N

FART!

...JUST SO I CAN BECOME DISTRACTED BY THE NFL PLAYOFFS AT THE END OF JANUARY, AND PLANT MYSELF RIGHT BACK IN THIS RECLINER FOR 11 MONTHS, WHILE TELLING MYSELF I'M IN BETTER SHAPE NOW THAN I WAS IN DECEMBER...

CHIPS

...SEE YOU ALL NEXT YEAR!

TV commercials for prescription drugs that tell you how effective the drug was at curing constipation in pregnant women over the age of forty-five who experienced a stroke, may have allergies, are nursing, pregnant, or may become pregnant. Side effects may include dry mouth, headache, or an alien fetus gestating in your stomach. Why do you have to tell me this if you already said go ask a damn doctor?

When you're driving down a highway in the left lane, and you pull into the right lane as you're about to pass an on-ramp. Then some jerk drifts down the ramp and stumbles out in front of you going forty mph.

How old people's houses are cluttered with so many pictures, plates, and vases that I feel like I'm going to break a half-dozen porcelain elephants and an urn if I turn around too fast.

Marathon runners who grab cups of water from someone, chug them, and then just toss the cups on the ground. Who do you expect to pick that up? Next time I'm going to stand down there and hold-out a cup full of vodka. Enjoy, litterbug.

When you want to do a quick software upgrade on your computer because it's been pestering you to do it for weeks, so you finally hit "OK." But then it ends up taking an hour and a half to finish, and also makes you restart the damn computer four times. For your information, I'd also be perfectly happy with the same version of your software I downloaded in 2001, so I don't need to be notified of an upgrade THREE TIMES A DAMN WEEK.

Why are menus at fast food drive-throughs displayed directly above the microphone where you place an order? Why isn't the menu visible to the next car in line so customers can decide what they want before they pull up to order? I never know what I want, and when I pull up to look at the menu, some zit-head is already lunging out the intercom at me.

When a televised sporting event goes into overtime, and they still show commercials. The sponsors have already received the allotted time they paid for, and any more is extra gravy. Overtime should be commercial free. Oh, and by this point, if someone has herpes, they probably know about Valtrex by now, so we don't all need to see the same commercial for your product eight times an hour.

When you go golfing, and you're packing your bag with beer cans, and you drop one of the cans, and it rolls ten feet away. Then you stroll up to the first hole and reach into your bag for a brew. Guess which one you pick?

When you're watching a football game on TV, but you're really following another game that's not being televised, so your eyes are glued to the out-of-town scoreboard. Yet instead of just briskly cycling through the scores one after another, they'll show a score, then spend five minutes showing the statistics of every player who caught a pass, ran for a yard, and threw up before the game. If the fantasy team I don't have was really that important, I'm sure I'd be glued to the Internet for updates. As for the folks with at least half a brain, is it that much to ask for simple, continuous, out-of-town scores?

Why is it so hard to find the trash can in a hotel room?

When you're watching a game on TV and the announcers already have the game's MVP picked with a good five minutes left to play. I always hope the other team's quarterback will lead a miraculous, three-touchdown comeback, and leave them with their thumbs up their asses in the booth.

Professional wrestling fans who bring signs to matches and expect to be seen. There are probably two and a half signs for each person in the crowd, and you can't read any of them. It's kind of like the car you see on the highway with so many bumper stickers on it that you can't read any of them, and when you drive past the driver's side and look in, you realize not reading them probably kept your IQ score in the triple digits.

Who plays the "Sims"? You're honestly going to sit there and tell me you watch fake people live life for you, and tell them what to do? Just go back to work at night. Seriously, if you're going to admit failure in general, then just go back to work.

Can we bury the hatchet in these self-swipe credit card machines? If they were meant to speed things up, they achieved the exact opposite result.   First of all, no one ever sees them at the checkout aisle to begin with. Then you try swiping your card in the machine four different ways, and everyone looks at you like a four year old with a pituitary defect trying to jam a square block through a round hole.

Then, when you finally swipe your card correctly, the clerk gets fed up and leans over to push all the buttons for you, and does it with a look like you're the eighty-fifth moron to do it that afternoon.

Last is the best part: the electronic signature. The sensors on the machine's touchpad might pick up North Korea's next atomic weapons test if it took place within twenty-eight feet of the touchpad. The first time you sign your name, the touchpad picks up about three marks, and it looks like pigeon shit scattered on the sidewalk. So the clerk has to reset everything and tells you to hold the pen upright this time. So you clasp the pen like a kid with a crayon, and this time you can read the letters, but realize it looks nothing like your personal signature and that a Labrador retriever could probably piss a comparable pattern in a snow bank. Have a nice day.

You know what's even more annoying than infomercials for overpriced shit? When you actually see something on an infomercial you want to buy, but they never put a damn phone number on the screen. They keep pushing the product and interviewing Mr. and Mrs. Slogart who used to spend hours waxing each other's backs with Popsicle sticks, but now they use Wonder Product to eliminate all their hair with a flick of a switch. The whole time, I'm just sitting there yelling, "I'm SOLD! Stop it! I don't even want the thing! Just stop showing pictures of hideous people!"

When you're watching a commercial on TV and they put up a clock in the corner of the screen that says how long you have to order before the special offer ends. Look, if your product had any positive attributes whatsoever, it would sell itself. The fact that you have to pressure naïve consumers into wanting it is lame at best.

Movie reviews that use the phrase "tour de force."

Back to the Future 2 could never have transpired the way it did. Once "old Biff" stole the time machine in 2016 and traveled back to 1955 to give himself the sports betting book he never could have returned to the same future from which he had originated. Once the book was delivered in 1955, the future would have forever been altered, and "old Biff" would only have been able to travel to the altered version of 2016. Please re-shoot all scenes in the movie from this point forward and submit them for my approval.

When you're eating nacho chips that are covered in cheese and meat and sour cream and salsa, and you get to the last chip, and it's so drenched and covered that there's no clean spot to pick it up with and there are no utensils in sight.

How lawyers on TV commercials always have their office shelves filled with a bunch of expensive-looking books in the background, but the guy talking is wearing an $80 suit.

Why do state authorities have the right to put "No turn on red" signs at any local traffic light that happens to fall on a state route? Justifying your job's existence by being an annoyance is like clogging a toilet and just walking away: at the end of the day, you're still an asshole.

When gas stations charge an extra 9/10 of a cent on every gallon.

Book covers where the asshole author's name is made intentionally larger than the title of the book.

Sean was born in Carmel, Indiana in 1983 and grew up in both Kettering, Ohio and New Canaan, Connecticut. He is a member of the New Canaan Country School Class of 1998, New Canaan High School Class of 2001, and the Syracuse University School of Architecture Class of 2006. He looks forward to a life in architecture, writing, and any way to be paid to complain.

Are You Serious? is currently an independent publication. Any word of mouth would increase the chances of me signing a publishing deal, which would be appreciated. For more information please visit **seanstadler.com**

www.ingramcontent.com/pod-product-compliance
Lightning Source LLC
Chambersburg PA
CBHW060920040426

42445CB00011B/720